# BRITISH POLITICAL LEADERS

## LECTOR HOUSE PUBLIC DOMAIN WORKS

This book is a result of an effort made by Lector House towards making a contribution to the preservation and repair of original classic literature. The original text is in the public domain in the United States of America, and possibly other countries depending upon their specific copyright laws.

In an attempt to preserve, improve and recreate the original content, certain conventional norms with regard to typographical mistakes, hyphenations, punctuations and/or other related subject matters, have been corrected upon our consideration. However, few such imperfections might not have been rectified as they were inherited and preserved from the original content to maintain the authenticity and construct, relevant to the work. The work might contain a few prior copyright references as well as page references which have been retained, wherever considered relevant to the part of the construct. We believe that this work holds historical, cultural and/or intellectual importance in the literary works community, therefore despite the oddities, we accounted the work for print as a part of our continuing effort towards preservation of literary work and our contribution towards the development of the society as a whole, driven by our beliefs.

We are grateful to our readers for putting their faith in us and accepting our imperfections with regard to preservation of the historical content. We shall strive hard to meet up to the expectations to improve further to provide an enriching reading experience.

Though, we conduct extensive research in ascertaining the status of copyright before redeveloping a version of the content, in rare cases, a classic work might be incorrectly marked as not-in-copyright. In such cases, if you are the copyright holder, then kindly contact us or write to us, and we shall get back to you with an immediate course of action.

**HAPPY READING!**

# BRITISH POLITICAL LEADERS

## JUSTIN MCCARTHY

ISBN: 978-93-5614-048-6

Published: 1903

© 2022
LECTOR HOUSE LLP

**LECTOR HOUSE LLP**
E-MAIL: lectorpublishing@gmail.com

*Photograph copyright by Elliott & Fry*
**ARTHUR JAMES BALFOUR**

# BRITISH POLITICAL LEADERS

BY

JUSTIN MCCARTHY

WITH PORTRAITS

1903

# CONTENTS

*Page*

| | |
|---|---|
| I. ARTHUR JAMES BALFOUR | 1 |
| II. LORD SALISBURY | 10 |
| III. LORD ROSEBERY | 19 |
| IV. JOSEPH CHAMBERLAIN | 28 |
| V. HENRY LABOUCHERE | 38 |
| VI. JOHN MORLEY | 47 |
| VII. THE EARL OF ABERDEEN | 56 |
| VIII. JOHN BURNS | 65 |
| IX. SIR MICHAEL HICKS-BEACH | 74 |
| X. JOHN E. REDMOND | 83 |
| XI. SIR WILLIAM HARCOURT | 92 |
| XII. JAMES BRYCE | 101 |
| XIII. SIR HENRY CAMPBELL-BANNERMAN | 110 |

# ARTHUR JAMES BALFOUR

My first acquaintance with Mr. Arthur J. Balfour, who recently became Prime Minister of King Edward VII., was made in the earliest days of my experience as a member of the House of Commons. The Fourth party, as it was called, had just been formed under the inspiration of the late Lord Randolph Churchill. The Fourth party was a new political enterprise. The House of Commons up to that time contained three regular and recognized political parties—the supporters of the Government, the supporters of the Opposition, and the members of the Irish Nationalist party, of whom I was one. Lord Randolph Churchill created a Fourth party, the business of which was to act independently alike of the Government, the Opposition, and the Irish Nationalists. At the time when I entered Parliament the Conservatives were in power, and Conservative statesmen occupied the Treasury Bench. The members of Lord Randolph's party were all Conservatives so far as general political principles were concerned, but Lord Randolph's idea was to lead a number of followers who should be prepared and ready to speak and vote against any Government proposal which they believed to be too conservative or not conservative enough; to support the Liberal Opposition in the rare cases when they thought the Opposition was in the right; and to support the Irish Nationalists when they believed that these were unfairly dealt with, or when they believed, which happened much more frequently, that to support the Irishmen would be an annoyance to the party in power.

The Fourth party was made up of numbers exactly corresponding with the title which had been given to it. Four men, including the leader, constituted the whole strength of this little army. These men were Lord Randolph Churchill, Arthur J. Balfour, John Gorst (now Sir John Gorst), and Sir Henry Drummond Wolff, who has during more recent years withdrawn altogether from parliamentary life and given himself up to diplomacy, in which he has won much honorable distinction. Sir John Gorst has recently held office in the Government, and is believed to have given and felt little satisfaction in his official career. He is a man of great ability and acquirements, but these have been somewhat thrown away in the business of administration.

The Fourth Party certainly did much to make the House of Commons a lively place. Its members were always in attendance—the whole four of them—and no one ever knew where, metaphorically, to place them. They professed and made manifest open scorn for the conventionalities of party life, and the parliamentary whips never knew when they could be regarded as supporters or opponents. They were all effective debaters, all ready with sarcasm and invective, all sworn foes to dullness and routine, all delighting in any opportunity for obstructing and bewildering the party which happened to be in power. The members of the Fourth party had each of them a distinct individuality, although they invariably acted together and were never separated in the division lobbies. A member of the House of Commons likened them once in a speech to D'Artagnan and his Three Musketeers, as pictured in the immortal pages of the elder Dumas. John Gorst he described as Porthos, Sir Henry Drummond Wolff as Athos, and Arthur Balfour as the sleek and subtle Aramis. When I entered Parliament I was brought much into companionship with the members of this interesting Fourth party. One reason for this habit of intercourse was that we sat very near to one another on the benches of the House. The members of the Irish Nationalist party then, as now, always sat on the side of the Opposition, no matter what Government happened to be in power, for the principle of the Irish Nationalists is to regard themselves as in perpetual opposition to every Government so long as Ireland is deprived of her own national legislature. Soon after I entered the House a Liberal Government was the result of a general election, and the Fourth party, as habitually conservative, sat on the Opposition benches. The Fourth party gave frequent support to the Irish Nationalists in their endeavors to resist and obstruct Government measures, and we therefore came into habitual intercourse, and even comradeship, with Lord Randolph Churchill and his small band of followers.

Arthur Balfour bore little resemblance, in appearance, in manners, in debating qualities, and apparently in mould of intellect, to any of the three men with whom he was then constantly allied. He was tall, slender, pale, graceful, with something of an almost feminine attractiveness in his bearing, although he was as ready, resolute, and stubborn a fighter as any one of his companions in arms. He had the appearance and the ways of a thoughtful student and scholar, and one would have associated him rather with a college library or a professor's chair than with the rough and boisterous ways of the House of Commons. He seemed to have come from another world of thought and feeling into that eager, vehement, and sometimes rather uproarious political assembly. Unlike his uncle, Lord Salisbury, he was known to enjoy social life, but he was especially given to that select order of æsthetic social life which was "sicklied o'er with the pale cast of thought," a form of life which was rather fashionable in society just then. But it must have been clear even to the most superficial observer that he had a decided gift of parliamentary capacity. He was a fluent and a ready speaker and could bear an effective part in any debate at a moment's notice, but he never declaimed, never indulged in any flight of eloquence, and seldom raised his clear and musical voice much above the conversational pitch. His choice of language was always happy and telling, and he often expressed himself in characteristic phrases which lived in the memory and passed into familiar quotation. He had won some distinction as a writer by his "Defense of Philosophic Doubt," by a volume of "Essays and Addresses," and more lately by his work entitled "The Foundations of Belief." The first and last of these books were inspired by a graceful and easy skepticism which had in it nothing particularly destructive to the faith of any believer, but aimed only at the not difficult task of proving that a doubting ingenuity can raise curious cavils from the practical and argumentative point of view against one creed as well as against another. The world did not take these skeptical ventures very seriously, and they were for the most part regarded as the attempts of a clever young man to show how much more clever he was than the ordinary run of believing mortals. Balfour's style was clear and vigorous, and people read the essays because of the writer's growing position in political life, and out of curiosity to see how the rising young statesman could display himself as the avowed advocate of philosophic skepticism.

Arthur Balfour took a conspicuous part in the attack made upon the Liberal Government in 1882 on the subject of the once famous Kilmainham Treaty. The action which he took in this instance was avowedly inspired by a desire to embarrass and oppose the Government because of the compromise into which it had endeavored to enter with Charles Stewart Parnell for some terms of agreement as to the manner in which legislation in Ireland ought to be administered. The full history of what was called the Kilmainham Treaty has not, so far as I know, been ever correctly given to the public, and it is not necessary, when surveying the political career of Mr. Balfour, to enter into any lengthened explanation on the subject. Mr. Parnell was in prison at the time when the arrangement was begun, and those who were in his confidence were well aware that he was becoming greatly alarmed as to the state of Ireland under the rule of the late W. E. Forster, who was then Chief Secretary to the Lord Lieutenant, and under whose operations leading Irishmen were thrown into prison on no definite charge, but because their general conduct left them open in the mind of the Chief Secretary to the suspicion that their public agitation was likely to bring about a rebellious movement. Parnell began to fear that the state of the country would become worse and worse if every popular movement were to be forcibly repressed at the time when the leaders in whom the Irish people had full confidence were kept in prison and their guidance, control, and authority withdrawn from the work of pacification. The proposed arrangement, whether begun by Mr. Parnell himself or suggested to him by members of his own party or of the English Radical party, was simply an understanding that if the leading Irishmen were allowed to return to their public work the country might at least be kept in peace while English Liberalism was devising some measures for the better government of Ireland. The arrangement was in every sense creditable alike to Parnell and to the English Liberals who were anxious to cooperate with him in such a purpose. But it led to some disturbance in Mr. Gladstone's government and to Mr. Forster's resignation of his office. In 1885, when the Conservatives again came into power and formed a government, Balfour was appointed President of the Local Government Board and afterwards became Chief Secretary to the Lord Lieutenant—in other words, Chief Secretary for Ireland. He had to attempt a difficult, or rather, it should be said, an impossible task, and he got through it about as well as, or as badly as, any other man could have done whose appointed mission was to govern Ireland on Tory principles for the interests of the landlords and by the policy of coercion.

Balfour, it should be said, was never, even at that time, actually unpopular with the Irish National party. We all understood quite well that his own heart did not go with the sort of administrative work which was put upon him; his manners were always courteous, agreeable, and graceful; he had a keen, quiet sense of humor, was on good terms personally with the leading Irish members, and never showed any inclination to make himself needlessly or wantonly offensive to his opponents. He was always readily accessible to any political opponent who had any suggestion to make, and his term of office as Chief Secretary, although of necessity quite unsuccessful for any practical good, left no memories of rancor behind it in the minds of those whom he had to oppose and to confront. More lately he became First Lord of the Treasury and Leader of the House of Commons, and the remainder of his public career is too well known to call for any detailed description here. My object in this article is rather to give a living picture of the man himself as we all saw him in public life than to record in historical detail the successive steps by which he ascended to his present high position, or rather, it should be said, of the successive events which brought that place within his reach and made it necessary for him to accept it. For it is only fair to say that, so far as outer observers could judge, Mr. Balfour never made his career a struggle for high positions. So clever and gifted a man must naturally have had some ambition in the public field to which he had devoted so absolutely his time and his talents. But he seemed, so far as one could judge, to have in him none of the self-seeking qualities which are commonly seen in the man whose purpose is to make his parliamentary work the means of arriving at the highest post in the government of the State. On the contrary, his whole demeanor seemed to be rather that of one who is devoting himself unwillingly to a career not quite congenial. He always appeared to me to be essentially a man of literary, scholarly, and even retiring tastes, who has a task forced upon him which he does not feel quite free to decline, and who therefore strives to make the best of a career which he has not chosen, but from which he does not feel at liberty to turn away. Most men who have attained the same political position give one the idea that they feel a positive delight in parliamentary life and warfare, and that nature must have designed them for that particular field and for none other. The joy in the strife which men like Palmerston, like Disraeli, and like Gladstone evidently felt never showed itself in the demeanor of Arthur Balfour. There was always something in his manner which spoke of a shy and shrinking disposition, and he never appeared to enter into debate for the mere pleasure of debating. He gave the idea of one who would much rather not make a speech were he altogether free to please himself in the matter, and as if he were only constraining himself to undertake a duty which most of those around him were but too glad to have an opportunity of attempting.

There are instances, no doubt, of men gifted with an absolute genius for eloquent speech who have had no natural inclination for debate and would rather have been free from any necessity for entering into the war of words. I have heard John Bright say that he would never make a speech if he did not feel it a duty imposed upon him, and that he would never enter the House of Commons if he felt free to keep away from its debates. Yet Bright was a born orator and was, on the whole, I think, the greatest public and parliamentary orator I have ever heard in England, not excluding even Gladstone himself. Bright had all the physical qualities of the orator. He had a commanding presence and a voice of the most marvelous intonation, capable of expressing in musical sound every emotion which lends itself to eloquence—the impassioned, the indignant, the pathetic, the appealing, and the humorous. Then I can recall an instance of another man, not, indeed, endowed with Bright's superb oratorical gifts, but who had to spend the greater part of his life since he attained the age of manhood in the making of speeches within and outside the House of Commons. I am thinking now of Charles Stewart Parnell. I know well that Parnell would never have made a speech if he could have avoided the task, and that he even felt a nervous dislike to the mere putting of a question in the House. But no one would have known from Bright's manner when he took part in a great debate that he was not obeying in congenial mood the full instinct and inclination of a born orator. Nor would a stranger have guessed from Parnell's clear, self-possessed, and precise style of speaking that he was putting a severe constraint upon himself when he made up his mind to engage in parliamentary debate. There is something in Arthur Balfour's manner as a speaker which occasionally reminds me of Parnell and his style. The two men had the same quiet, easy, and unconcerned fashion of utterance, always choosing the most appropriate word and finding it without apparent difficulty; each man seemed, as I have already said of Balfour, to be thinking aloud rather than trying to convince the listeners; each man spoke as if resolved not to waste any words or to indulge in any appeal to the mere emotions of the audience. But the natural reluctance to take any part in debate was always more conspicuous in the manner of Balfour than even in that of Parnell.

Balfour is a man of many and varied tastes and pursuits. He is an advocate of athleticism and is especially distinguished for his devotion to the game of golf. He obtained at one time a certain reputation in London society because of the interest he took in some peculiar phases of fanciful intellectual inventiveness. He was for a while a leading member, if not the actual inventor, of a certain order of psychical research whose members were described as The Souls. More than one novelist of the day made picturesque use of this singular order and enlivened the pages of fiction by fancy portraits of its leading members. Such facts as these did much to prevent Balfour from being associated in the public mind with only the rivalries of political parties and the incidents of parliamentary warfare. One sometimes came into social circles where Balfour was regarded chiefly as the man of literary tastes and somewhat eccentric intellectual developments. All this cast a peculiar reflection over his career as a politician and filled many observers with the idea that he was only playing at parliamentary life, and that his other occupations were the genuine realities for him. Even to this day there are some who persist in believing that Balfour, despite his prolonged and unvarying attention to his parliamentary duties, has never given his heart to the prosaic and practical work of administrative office and the business of maintaining his political party. Yet it has always had to be acknowledged that no man attended more carefully and more closely to such work when he had to do it, and that the most devoted worshiper of political success could not have been more regular and constant in his attention to the business of the House of Commons. People said that he was lazy by nature, that he loved long hours of sleep and of general rest, and that he detested the methodical and mechanical routine of official work. But I have not known any Minister of State who was more easy of approach and more ready to enter into the driest details of departmental business than Arthur Balfour. I may say, too, that, whenever appeal was made to him to forward any good work or to do any act of kindness, he was always to be found at his post and was ever ready to lend a helping hand if he could.

I remember one instance of this kind which I have no hesitation in mentioning, although I am quite sure Mr. Balfour had little inclination for its obtaining publicity. Not very many years ago it was brought to my knowledge that an English literary woman who had won much and deserved distinction as a novel-writer had been for some time sinking into ill health, had been therefore prevented from going on with her work, and had in the mean time been perplexed by worldly difficulties and embarrassments which interfered sadly with her prospects and made her a subject of well-merited sympathy. Some friends of the authoress were naturally anxious, if possible, to give her a helping hand, and the idea occurred to them that she would be a most fitting recipient of assistance to be bestowed by a department of the State. One of her friends, himself a distinguished novelist, who happened to be also a friend of mine, spoke to me with this object, assuming that, as an old parliamentary hand, I knew more than most writers of books would be likely to know about the manner in which such help might be obtained. There is in England a fund—a very small fund, truly—at the disposal of the Government for the help of deserving authors who happen to be in distress. This fund is at the disposal of the First Lord of the Treasury, the office which was then, as now, held by Arthur Balfour. I was still at that time a member of the House of Commons, and my friend suggested that, as I knew something about the whole business, I might be a suitable person to represent the case to the First Lord of the Treasury and make appeal for his assistance. My friend's belief was that the application might come with more effect from one who had been for a long time a member of Parliament, and whose name would therefore be known to the First Lord of the Treasury, than from a literary man who had nothing to do with parliamentary life. Nothing could give me greater pleasure than to become the medium through which the appeal might be brought under the notice of the First Lord, but I felt some difficulty and doubt because of the conditions of the time. England was then in the most distracting period of the South African war. We were hearing every day of fresh mishaps and disasters in the campaign. Arthur Balfour was Leader of the House of Commons, and had to deal every day with questions, with demands for explanation, with arguments and debates turning on the events of the war. It seemed to me to be rather a venturesome enterprise to attempt to gain the attention of a minister thus perplexingly occupied for a matter of merely private and individual concern. I feared that an overworked statesman might feel naturally inclined to remit the subject to the care of some mere official, and that time might thus be lost and the needed helping hand be long delayed. I undertook the task, however, and I wrote to Mr. Balfour at once. I received the very next day a reply written in Mr. Balfour's own hand, expressing his cordial willingness to consider the subject, his sympathy with the purpose of the appeal, and his hope that some help might be given to the distressed novelist. Mr. Balfour promptly took the matter in hand, and the result was that a grant was made from the State fund to secure the novelist against any actual distress. Now, I do not want to make too much of this act of ready kindness done by Mr. Balfour. The appeal was made for a most deserving object; the fund from which help was to be given was entirely at Mr. Balfour's disposal; and it is probable that any other First Lord in the same circumstances would have come to the same decision. But how easy it would have been for Mr. Balfour to put the whole matter into the hands of some subordinate, and not to add a new trouble to his own intensely busy life at such an exciting crisis by entering into the close consideration of a mere question of State beneficence! I certainly should not have been surprised if I had not received an answer to my letter for several days after I had sent it, and if even then it had come from some subordinate in the Government department. But in the midst of all his incessant and distracting occupations at a most exciting period of public business Mr. Balfour found time to consider the question himself, to reply with his own hand, and to see that the desired help was promptly accorded. I must say that I think this short passage of personal history speaks highly for the kindly nature and the sympathetic promptitude of Arthur Balfour.

For a long time there had been much speculation in these countries concerning the probable successor to Lord Salisbury, whenever Lord Salisbury should make up his mind to resign the position of Prime Minister. We all knew that that resignation was sure to come soon, although very few of us had any idea that it was likely to come quite so soon. The general opinion was that the country would not be expected, for some time at least, to put up again with a Prime Minister in the House of Lords. If, therefore, the new Prime Minister had to be found in the House of Commons, there seemed to be only a choice between two men, Arthur Balfour and Joseph Chamberlain. It would be hard to find two men in the House of Commons more unlike each other in characteristic qualities and in training than these two. They are both endowed with remarkable capacity for political life and for parliamentary debate, "but there," as Byron says concerning two of whom one was a Joseph, "I doubt all likeness ends between the pair." Balfour is an aristocrat of aristocrats; Chamberlain is essentially a man of the British middle class—even what is generally called the lower middle class. Balfour has gone through all the regular course of university education; Chamberlain was for a short time at University College School in London, a popular institution of modern origin which does most valuable educational work, but is not largely patronized by the classes who claim aristocratic position. Balfour is a constant reader and student of many literatures and languages; "Mr. Chamberlain," according to a leading article in a London daily newspaper, "to put it mildly, is not a bookworm." Balfour loves open-air sports and is a votary of athleticism; Chamberlain never takes any exercise, even walking exercise, when he can possibly avoid the trouble. Balfour is an æsthetic lover of all the arts; Chamberlain has never, so far as I know, given the slightest indication of interest in any artistic subject. Balfour is by nature a modest and retiring man; Chamberlain is always "Pushful Joe." The stamp and character of a successful municipal politician are always evident in Chamberlain, while Balfour seems to be above all other things the university scholar and member of high society. I suppose it must have been a profound disappointment to Chamberlain that he was not offered the place of Prime Minister, but it would be hardly fair to expect that such a place would not be offered to the First Lord of the Treasury and Leader of the House of Commons, even if that First Lord did not happen to be a nephew of the retiring Prime Minister.

It would be idle just now to enter into any speculation as to whether Mr. Arthur Balfour will long continue to hold the office. If he should make up his mind, as was at one time thought possible by many observers, to accept a peerage and become Prime Minister in the House of Lords, such a step would undoubtedly be a means of pacifying the partisans of Chamberlain, for Chamberlain would then become, almost as a matter of course, the leader of the Conservative government in the House of Commons, and this elevation might well satisfy his ambition and give his pushful energy work enough to do. But the country has of late become less and less satisfied with the practice of having a Prime Minister removed from the centre of active life and hidden away in the enervating atmosphere of the House of Lords. The friends of Mr. Balfour are naturally inclined to hope and believe that he will not bury himself in such a living tomb. His path will in any case be perplexed by many difficulties and obstructions. My own impression is that the inevitable reaction is destined to come before long. The next general election may prove that the country at large is tired of a Conservative administration. The public mind will soon get over the feverish excitement created by the South African war, and people will begin to remember that England had won battles and annexed territory before there ever was a Transvaal Republic, and found then, as she will find now, that successes abroad do not relieve her from the necessity of managing successfully her business at home. It has to be borne in mind, too, that the House of Commons does not really originate anything in the work of important legislation. The best business of the Liberal party begins outside the House of Commons—begins with the people and with those who take an interest in the welfare of the people and have brains and foresight enough to find out how it can be most thoroughly promoted. All great reforms have their origin outside the House of Commons and are only taken up by the House of Commons when it is felt that the popular demand is so earnest that it must receive serious consideration. The country will soon begin to realize the fact that, shamefully mismanaged as the War Department may have been during the recent campaigns, the War Department is not by any means the only national institution which needs the strong hand of reform. The spirited foreign policy has had its innings, and the condition of the people at home must have its turn very soon. The Liberal party has its work cut out for it, and where there is the work to be done a Liberal party will be found to do it. So far as I can read the signs of the times, I am encouraged to hope that a great opportunity is waiting for the Liberal party, and I cannot see the slightest reason to doubt that a Liberal party will be found ready for the opportunity and equal to it. A Tory Prime Minister has, indeed, before now had the judgment and the energy to forestall the Liberal party in the great work of domestic reform, but I do not believe that even the warmest admirers of Mr. Balfour imagine that he is quite the man to undertake such an enterprise. Arthur Balfour is, according to my judgment, the best man for the place to be found in the Conservative ranks at present, but I do not suppose that he is destined just now to be anything more than a stop-gap. I admire his great and varied abilities, I recognize his brilliant debating powers, and I have felt the charm of his genial and graceful manners, but I do not believe him capable of maintaining the present administration against the rising force of a Liberal reaction.

*From a painting by Hubert von Herkomer*
**LORD SALISBURY**

# LORD SALISBURY

The retirement of Lord Salisbury from the position of Prime Minister and the leadership of the Conservative Government withdraws into comparative obscurity the most interesting and even picturesque figure in the English Parliamentary life of the present day. Even the most uncompromising opponents of the Prime Minister and of his political party felt a sincere respect for the character, the intellect, and the bearing of the man himself. Every one gave Lord Salisbury full credit for absolute sincerity of purpose, for superiority to any personal ambitions or mere self-seeking, for an almost contemptuous disregard of State honors and political fame.

Yet it was not that Lord Salisbury was habitually careful and measured in his speech, that he was never hurried into rash utterances, that he was guided by any particular anxiety to avoid offending the susceptibilities of others, or, indeed, that, as a rule, he preferred to use soothing words in political controversy. He has, on the contrary, a marvelous gift of sarcasm and of satirical phrase-making, and he was only too ready to indulge occasionally this peculiar capacity at the expense of political friend as well as of political foe. In his early days of public life, when he sat in the House of Commons as a nominal follower of Mr. Disraeli, he was once described in debate by his nominal leader as "a master of flouts and jeers." On another occasion Disraeli spoke of him, although not in Parliamentary debate, as a young man whose head was on fire. In later days, and even when he had held high administrative office, Lord Salisbury often indulged in sudden outbursts of contemptuous humor which for a time seemed likely to provoke indignant remonstrance even from his own followers. One illustration of this unlucky tendency towards contemptuous utterance may be found in his famous allusion several years ago to a native of Hindustan, who had been elected to a seat in the House of Commons, as "a black man." That was a time when every English public man recognized the great importance of indulging in no expression which might seem calculated to wound the susceptibilities of the many races who have been brought under the rule of the Imperial system in the Indian dominions of the sovereign. The member of Parliament thus scornfully alluded to was no more a black man than Lord Salisbury himself. He was one of the Parsee races chiefly found in the Bombay regions, almost European in the color of their skin, and he looked more like a German scholar than a native of any sunburnt land. No one defended Lord Salisbury's rash utterance, but many people excused it on the ground that it was only Lord Salisbury's way; that he never meant any harm, but could not resist the temptation of saying an amusing and sarcastic thing when it came into his mind. The truth is that Lord Salisbury's odd humor is a peculiarity without which he could not be the complete Lord Salisbury, and an unlucky expression was easily forgiven because of the many brilliant flashes of genuine and not unfair sarcasm with which he was accustomed to illumine a dull debate. When he succeeded to his father's title, and had, therefore, to leave the House of Commons and take his place in the House of Lords, every one felt that the representative chamber had lost one of its most attractive figures, and that the hereditary chamber was not exactly the place in which such a man could find his happiest hunting-ground. Yet even in the somber and unimpressive House of Lords, Lord Salisbury was able, whenever the humor took him, to brighten the debates by his apt illustrations and his witty humor.

Lord Salisbury resigns his position as Prime Minister at a time of life when, according to the present standards of age, a man is still supposed to have long years of good work before him. Lord Palmerston's career as Prime Minister was cut short only by his death, an event which occurred when Palmerston was in his eighty-first year. Gladstone was more than ten years older than Lord Salisbury is now when he voluntarily gave up his position as head of a Liberal administration. Lord Beaconsfield's time of birth is somewhat uncertain, but he must have been some seventy-seven years of age and had lost none of his powers as a debater when his brilliant life came to its close. We may take it for granted that Lord Salisbury had been for a long time growing tired of the exalted political position which had of late become uncongenial with his habits and his frame of mind. By the death of his wife he had lost the most loved companion of his home, his intellectual tastes, and his political career. A pair more thoroughly devoted to each other than Lord and Lady Salisbury could hardly have been found even in the pages of romance. The whole story of that marriage and that married life would have supplied a touching and a telling chapter for romance. Early in his public career Lord Salisbury fell in love with a charming, gifted, and devoted woman, whom a happy chance had brought in his way. She was the daughter of an eminent English judge, the late Baron Alderson; and although such a wife might have been thought a suitable match even for a great aristocrat, it appears that the Lord Salisbury of that time, the father of the late Prime Minister, who was then only Lord Robert Cecil, did not approve of the marriage, and the young pair had to take their own way and become husband and wife without regard for the family prejudices. Lord Robert Cecil was then only a younger brother with a younger brother's allowance to live on, and the newly wedded pair had not much of a prospect before them, in the conventional sense of the words. Lord Robert Cecil accepted the situation with characteristic courage and resolve. There seemed at that time no likelihood of his ever succeeding to the title and the estates, for his elder brother was living, and was, of course, heir to the ancestral title and property. Lord Robert Cecil had been gifted with distinct literary capacity, and he set himself down to work as a writer and a journalist. He became a regular contributor to the "Saturday Review," then at the height of its influence and fame, and he wrote articles for some of the ponderous quarterly reviews of the time, brightening their pages by his animated and forcible style. He took a small house in a modest quarter of London, where artists and poets and authors of all kinds usually made a home then, far removed from West End fashion and courtly splendor, and there he lived a happy and productive life for many years. He had obtained a seat in the House of Commons as a member of the Conservative party, but he never pledged himself to support every policy and every measure undertaken by the Conservative leaders, whether they happened to be in or out of office. Lord Robert always acted as an independent member, although he adhered conscientiously to the cardinal principles of that Conservative doctrine which was his political faith throughout his life. He soon won for himself a marked distinction in the House of Commons. He was always a brilliant speaker, but was thoughtful and statesmanlike as well as brilliant. He never became an orator in the higher sense of the word. He never attempted any flights of exalted eloquence. His speeches were like the utterances of a man who is thinking aloud and whose principal object is to hold and convince his listeners by the sheer force of argument set forth in clear and telling language. Many of his happy phrases found acceptance as part of the ordinary language of political and social life and became in their way immortal. Up to the present day men are continually quoting happy phrases drawn from Lord Robert Cecil's early speeches without remembering the source from which they came.

Such a capacity as that of Lord Robert Cecil could not long be overlooked by the leaders of his party, and it soon became quite clear that he must be invited to administrative office. I ought to say that, after Lord Robert had completed his collegiate studies at Oxford, he devoted himself for a considerable time to an extensive course of travel, and he visited Australasia, then but little known to young Englishmen of his rank, and he actually did much practical work as a digger in the Australian gold mines, then newly discovered. He had always a deep interest in foreign affairs, and it was greatly to the advantage of his subsequent career that he could often support his arguments on questions of foreign policy by experience drawn from a personal study of the countries and States forming successive subjects of debate. Suddenly his worldly prospects underwent a complete change. The death of his elder brother made him heir to the family title and the great estates. He became Viscount Cranborne in succession to his dead brother. I may perhaps explain, for the benefit of some of my American readers, that the heir to a peerage who bears what is called a courtesy title has still a right to sit, if elected, in the House of Commons. It is sometimes a source of wonder and puzzlement to foreign visitors when they find so many men sitting in the House of Commons who actually bear titles which would make it seem as if they ought to be in the House of Lords. The eldest sons of all the higher order of peers bear such a title, but it carries with it no disqualification for a seat in the House of Commons, if the bearer of it be duly elected to a place in the representative chamber. When the bearer of the courtesy title succeeds to the actual title belonging to the house, he then, as a matter of course, becomes a peer, has to enter the House of Lords, and would no longer be legally eligible to sit in the representative chamber. Lord Palmerston's presence in the House of Commons was often a matter of wonder to foreign visitors, for in all the days to which my memory goes back, Lord Palmerston seemed too old a man to have a father alive and in the House of Lords. I have had to explain the matter to many a stranger, and it only gives one other illustration of the peculiarities and anomalies which belong to our Parliamentary system. Palmerston's was not a courtesy title; the noble lord was a peer in his own right; but then he was merely an

Irish peer, and only a certain number of Irish peers are entitled to sit in the House of Lords. The more fortunate, for so I must describe them, of the Irish peers not thus entitled to sit in the hereditary chamber are free to seek election for an English constituency in the House of Commons and to obtain it, as Lord Palmerston did. Lord Viscount Cranborne, therefore, continued for a time to hold the place in the House of Commons which he had held as Lord Robert Cecil. In 1866 Lord Cranborne entered office, for the first time, as Secretary of State for India during the administration of Lord Derby.

The year following brought about a sort of crisis in Lord Cranborne's political career, and probably showed the general public of England, for the first time, what manner of man he really was. Up to that period he had been regarded by most persons, even among those who habitually gave attention to Parliamentary affairs, as a brilliant, independent, and somewhat audacious free-lance whose political conduct was usually directed by the impulse of the moment, and who made no pretensions to any fixed and ruling principles. That was the year 1867, when the Conservative Government under Lord Derby and Mr. Disraeli took it into their heads to try the novel experiment, for a Conservative party, of introducing a Reform Bill to improve and expand the conditions of the Parliamentary suffrage. Disraeli was the author of this new scheme, and it had been suggested to him by Mr. Gladstone's failure in the previous year with his measure of reform. Gladstone's reform measure did not go far enough to satisfy the genuine Radicals, while it went much too far for a considerable number of doubtful and half-hearted Liberals, and it was strongly opposed by the whole Tory party. As usually happens in the case of every reform introduced by a Liberal administration, a secession took place among the habitual followers of the Government. The secession in this case was made famous by the name which Bright conferred upon it as the "Cave of Adullam" party; and by the co-operation of the seceding section with the Tory Opposition, the measure was defeated, and Mr. Gladstone went out of office. Disraeli saw, with his usual sagacity, that the vast mass of the population were in favor of some measure of reform, and when Lord Derby and he came into office he made up his mind that, as the thing had to be done, he and his colleagues might as well have the advantage of doing it. The outlines of the measure prepared for the purpose only shaped a very vague and moderate scheme of reform, but Disraeli was quite determined to accept any manner of compromises in order to carry some sort of scheme and to keep himself and his party in power. But then arose a new difficulty on which, with all his sagacity, he had not calculated. Lord Cranborne for the first time showed that he was a man of clear and resolute political principle, and that he was not willing to sacrifice any of his conscientious convictions for the sake of maintaining his place in a Government. He was sincerely opposed to every project for making the suffrage popular and for admitting the mass of the workingmen of the country to any share in its government. I need hardly say that I am entirely opposed to Lord Cranborne's political theories, but I am none the less willing to render full justice to the sincerity, not too common among rising public men, which refused to make any compromise on a matter of political principle. Lord Cranborne was then only at the opening of his administrative career, and he must have had personal ambition enough to make him wish for a continuance of office in a powerful administration. But he put all personal considerations resolutely aside, and resigned his place in the Government rather than have anything to do with a project which he believed to be a surrender of constitutional principle to the demands of the growing democracy. Lord Carnarvon and one or two other members of the administration followed his lead and resigned their places in the Government. I need not enter into much detail as to the progress of the Disraeli reform measure. It is enough to say that Disraeli obtained the support of many Radicals by the Liberal amendments which he accepted, and the result was that a Tory Government carried to success a scheme of reform which practically amounted to the introduction of household suffrage. Lord Cranborne and those who acted with him held firmly to their principles, and steadily opposed the measure introduced by those who at the opening of the session were their official leaders and colleagues. I am convinced that even the most advanced reformers were ready to give a due meed of praise to the man who had thus made it evident that he preferred what he believed to be a political principle, even though he knew it to be the principle of a losing cause, to any consideration of personal advancement.

Some of us felt sure that we had then learned for the first time what manner of man Lord Cranborne really was. We had taken him for a bold and brilliant adventurer, and we found and were ready to acknowledge that he was a man of deep, sincere, and self-sacrificing convictions. I have never from that time changed my opinions with regard to Lord Cranborne's personal character. His career interested me from the first moment that I had an opportunity of observing it, and I may say that from an early period of my manhood I had much opportunity of studying the ways and the figures of Parliamentary life. But until Lord Cranborne had taken this resolute position on the reform question, I had never given him credit for any depth of political convictions. The impression I formed of him up to that time was that he was merely a younger son of a great aristocratic family, who had a natural aptitude alike for literature and for politics, and that he was following in Parliament the guidance of his own personal humors and argumentative impulses, and that he was ready to sacrifice in debate not only his friends but his party for the sake of saying a clever thing and startling his audience into reluctant admiration. From those days of 1867 I knew him to be what all the world now knows him to be, a man of deep and sincere convictions, ever following the light of what he believes to be political wisdom and justice. I can say this none the less readily because I suppose it has hardly ever been my fortune to agree with any of Lord Salisbury's utterances on questions of political importance.

In 1868 the career of Lord Cranborne in the House of Commons came to an end by the death of his father. He succeeded to the title of Marquis of Salisbury, and became, as a matter of course, a member of the House of Lords. He was thus withdrawn while still a comparatively young man from that stirring field of splendid debate where his highest qualities as a speaker could alone have found their fitting opportunity. I need not trace out his subsequent public career with any sequence of detail. We all know how from that time to this he has held high office, has come to hold the highest offices in the State whenever his political party happened to be in power. He has been Foreign Secretary; he has been Prime Minister in three Conservative administrations. For a time he actually combined the functions of Prime Minister and those of Foreign Secretary. He was envoy to the great conference at Constantinople in 1876 and 1877, and he took part in the Congress of Berlin, that conference which Lord Beaconsfield declared brought to England peace with honor. Everything that a man could have to gratify his ambition Lord Salisbury has had since the day when he succeeded to his father's title and estates. His own intellectual force and his political capacity must undoubtedly have made a way for him to Parliamentary influence and success even if he had always remained Lord Robert Cecil, and his elder brother had lived to succeed to the title. But from the moment when Lord Robert Cecil became the heir, it was certain that his party could not venture to overlook him. He might have made eccentric speeches, he might have indulged in sarcastic and scornful allusions to his political leaders, he might have allowed obtrusive scruples of conscience to interfere with the interests of his party, but none the less it became absolutely necessary that the Conservative politicians should accept, when opportunity came, the leadership of the Marquis of Salisbury. "Thou hast it all"—the words which Banquo applies to Macbeth—might have been said of Lord Salisbury when he became for the first time Prime Minister.

Lord Salisbury certainly did not achieve his position by any of the arts, even the less culpable arts, which for a time secured to Macbeth the highest reach of his ambition. Lord Salisbury's leadership came to him and was not sought by him. I cannot help thinking, however, that, after he had once attained that supreme position in his party, the remainder of his public career has been something in the nature of an anticlimax. Was it that the chill and deadening influence of the House of Lords proved too depressing for the energetic and vivacious spirit which had won celebrity for Lord Robert Cecil in the House of Commons? Was it that Lord Salisbury, when he had attained the height of his ambition, became a victim to that mood of reaction which compels such a man to ask himself whether, after all, the work of ascent was not much better than the attained elevation? Lord Salisbury's years of high office coming now thus suddenly to an end give to me at least the melancholy impression of an unfulfilled career. The influence of the Prime Minister, so far as mere outsiders can judge of it, has always been exerted in foreign affairs for the promotion of peace. Even the late war in South Africa is not understood to have been in any sense a war of his seeking. The general belief is that the policy of war was pressed upon him by influences which at the time he was not able to control—influences which would only have become all the stronger if he had refused to accept the responsibility of Prime Minister and had left it to others to carry on the work of government. However this may be, it can hardly be questioned that of late years Lord Salisbury had become that which nobody in former days could ever suppose him likely to become, the mere figurehead of an administration. Lord Salisbury's whole nature seems to have been too sincere, too free from mere theatrical arts, to allow him to play the part of leader where he had no heart in the work of leadership. A statesman like Disraeli might have disapproved of a certain policy and done his best to reason his colleagues out of it, but nevertheless, when he found himself likely to be overborne, would have immersed himself deliberately in all the new-born zeal of the convert and would have behaved thenceforward as if his whole soul were in the work which had been put upon him to do. Lord Salisbury is most assuredly not a man of this order, and he never would or could put on an enthusiasm which he did not feel in his heart. We can all remember how, at the very zenith of British passion against China during the recent political convulsions and the intervention of the foreign allies, Lord Salisbury astonished and depressed some of his warmest admirers by a speech which he made at Exeter Hall, a speech which, metaphorically at least, threw the coldest of cold water on the popular British ardor for forcing Western civilization on the Chinese people.

Lord Salisbury's frame of mind was one which could never allow him to become even for a moment a thorough Jingo, and through all the later years of his power he held the office of Prime Minister at a time when Jingoism was the order of the day among the outside supporters of the Conservative Government. He never had a fair chance for the full development of his intellectual faculties while he remained at the head of a Conservative administration. Under happier conditions he might have been a great Prime Minister and a leading force in political movement, but his intellect, his tastes, and his habits of life did not allow him to pay much deference to the prejudices and passions of those on whom he was compelled to rely for support. There was too much in him of the thinker, the scholar, and the recluse to make him a thoroughly effective leader of the party who had to acknowledge his command. He loved reading, he loved literature and art, and he took no delight in the formal social functions which are in our days an important part of successful political administration. He could not be "hail-fellow-well-met" with every pushing follower who made it a pride to be on terms of companionship with the leader of the party. I have often heard that he had a singularly bad memory for faces, and that many a devoted Tory follower found his enthusiasm chilled every now and then by the obvious fact that the Prime Minister did not seem to remember anything about the identity of his obtrusive admirer. Much the same thing has been said over and over again about Mr. Gladstone, but then Gladstone had the inborn genius of leadership, threw his soul into every great political movement, and did not depend in the slightest degree on his faculty for appreciating and conciliating every individual follower. Lord Salisbury's tastes were for the society of his close personal friends, and I believe no man could be a more genial host in the company of those with whom he loved to associate; but he had no interest in the ordinary ways of society and made no effort to conciliate those with whom he found himself in no manner of companionship. He did not even take any strong interest in the study of the most remarkable figures in the political world around him, if he did not feel drawn into sympathy with their ways and their opinions. On one occasion, when a report had got about in the newspapers that Lord Salisbury was often seen in friendly companionship with the late Mr. Parnell in the smoking-room of the House of Commons, Lord Salisbury publicly stated that he had never, to his knowledge, seen Parnell, and had never been once in the House of Commons smoking-room.

No man has been better known, so far as personal appearance was concerned, to the general English public than Lord Salisbury. He has been as well known as

Mr. Gladstone himself, and one cannot say more than that. He was a frequent walker in St. James's Park and other places of common resort in the neighborhood of the Houses of Parliament. Every one knew the tall, broad, stooping figure with the thick head of hair, the bent brows, and the careless, shabby costume. No statesman of his time was more indifferent than Lord Salisbury to the dictates of fashion as regarded dress and deportment. He was undoubtedly one of the worst-dressed men of his order in London. In this peculiarity he formed a remarkable contrast to Lord Beaconsfield, who down to the very end of his life took care to be always dressed according to the most recent dictates of fashion. All this was strictly in keeping with Lord Salisbury's character and temperament. The world had to take him as he was—he could never bring himself to act any part for the sake of its effect upon the public. My own impression is that when he was removed by the decree of fate into the House of Lords and taken away from the active, thrilling life of the House of Commons, he felt himself excluded from his congenial field of political action and had but little interest in the game of politics any more. He does not seem destined to a place in the foremost rank of English Prime Ministers, even of English Conservative Prime Ministers. But his is beyond all question a picturesque, a deeply interesting, and even a commanding figure in English political history, and the world will have reason to regret if his voluntary retirement from the position of Prime Minister should mean also his retirement from the field of political life.

*Photograph copyright by Elliott & Fry*
**THE EARL OF ROSEBERY**

# LORD ROSEBERY

Lord Rosebery was for a prolonged season the man in English political life upon whom the eyes of expectation were turned. He is a younger man than most of his political colleagues and rivals, but it is not because of his comparative youth that the eyes of expectation were and still are turned upon him. Not one of those who stand in the front ranks of Parliamentary life to-day could be called old, as we reckon age in our modern estimate. Palmerston, Gladstone, and Disraeli won their highest political triumphs after they had passed the age which Lord Salisbury and Sir William Harcourt have now reached; Mr. Balfour is still regarded in politics as quite a young man, and Sir Henry Campbell-Bannerman has but lately been elected leader of the Liberal party in the House of Commons. Lord Rosebery has already held the highest political offices. He has been Foreign Secretary and he has been Prime Minister. He has been leader of the Liberal party. No other public man in England has so many and so varied mental gifts, and no other public man has won success in so many distinct fields. We live in days when, for the time at least, the great political orator seems to have passed out of existence. The last great English orator died at Hawarden a few short years ago. We have, however, several brilliant and powerful Parliamentary debaters, and among these Lord Rosebery stands with the foremost, if he is not, indeed, absolutely the foremost. As an orator on what I may call great ceremonial occasions he is, according to my judgment, the very foremost we now have. As an after-dinner speaker—and after-dinner speaking counts for a great deal in the success of an English public man—he has never had an equal in England during my time. Then Lord Rosebery has delivered lectures or addresses in commemoration of great poets and philosophers and statesmen which may even already be regarded as certain of an abiding place in literature. Lord Rosebery is a literary man, an author as well as a statesman and an orator; he has written a life of Pitt which is already becoming a sort of classic in our libraries. There are profounder students, men more deeply read, than he, but I doubt if there are many men living who have so wide an acquaintance with general literature. He is a lover as well as a student and a connoisseur of art, he is an accomplished yachtsman, has a thorough knowledge of horses, is famous on the turf, and the owner of two horses which won the Derby. The legendary fairy godmother seems to have showered upon him at his birth all her richest and most various gifts, and no malign and jealous sprite appears to have come in, as in the nursery stories, to spoil any of the gifts by a counteracting spell. He was born of great family and born to high estate; he married a daughter of the house of Rothschild; he has a lordly home near Edinburgh in Scotland, a noble house in the finest West End square of London, and a delightful residence in one of our most beautiful English counties.

Lord Rosebery is one of the most charming talkers whom it has ever been my good fortune to meet. He has a keen sense of humor, a happy art of light and delicate satire, and, in private conversation as well as in Parliamentary debate, he has a singular facility for the invention of expressive and successful phrases which tell their whole story in a flash. One might well be inclined to ask what the kindly fates could have done for Lord Rosebery that they have left undone. Nevertheless, the truth has to be told, that up to this time Lord Rosebery has not accomplished as much of greatness as most of us confidently expected that he would achieve.

I have been, perhaps, somewhat too hasty in saying that no counteracting spell had in any way marred the influence of the gifts which the fairies had so lavishly bestowed on Lord Rosebery. One stroke of ill fortune—ill fortune, that is, for an English political leader—was certainly directed against him. Nature must have meant him to be a successful Prime Minister, and yet fortune denied him a seat in the House of Commons. He succeeded to his grandfather's peerage at an early period of his life, and he had to begin his political career as a member of the House of Lords. He therefore missed all that splendid training for political warfare which is given in the House of Commons. It would not, perhaps, be quite easy for an American reader to understand how little the House of Lords counts for in the education of fighting statesmen.

When Charles James Fox was told in his declining years that the King, as a mark of royal favor, intended to make him a peer and thus remove him from the House of Commons into the House of Lords, he struck his forehead and exclaimed: "Good Heaven! he does not think it has come to that with me, does he?" Fox had had all the training that his genius needed in the House of Commons, and he was not condemned to pass into the House of Lords. Nothing but the inborn consciousness of a genius for political debate can stimulate a man to great effort in the House of Lords. Nothing turns upon a debate in that House. If a majority in the House of Lords were to pass a vote of censure three times a week on the existing Government, that Government would continue to exist just as if nothing had happened, and the public in general would hardly know that the Lords had been expressing any opinion on the subject. An ordinary sitting of the House of Lords is not expected to last for more than an hour or so, and the whole assembly often consists of some half a dozen peers. Now and again, during the course of a session, there is got up what may be called a full-dress debate when some great question is disturbing the country, and the peers think that they ought to put on the appearance of being deeply concerned about it, and some noble lord who has a repute for wisdom or for eloquence gives notice of a formal motion, and then there is a lengthened discussion, and perhaps, on some extraordinary occasion, the peers may sit to a late hour and even take a division. But on such remarkable occasions the peer who induces the House to come together and listen to his oration is almost sure to be one who has had his training in the House of Commons and has made his fame as an orator there.

Now, I cannot but regard it as a striking evidence of Lord Rosebery's inborn fitness to be an English political leader that he should have got over the dreary discouragement of such a training-school, and should have practiced the art of political oratory under conditions that might have filled Demosthenes himself with a sense of the futility of trying to make a great speech where nothing whatever was likely to come of it. Lord Rosebery, however, did succeed in proving to the House of Lords that they had among them a brilliant and powerful debater who had qualified himself for success without any help from the school in which Lord Brougham and the brilliant Lord Derby, Lord Cairns, and Lord Salisbury had studied and mastered the art of Parliamentary eloquence.

But, indeed, Lord Rosebery appears to have had a natural inclination to seek and find a training-school for his abilities in places and pursuits that might have seemed very much out of the ordinary British aristocrat's way. Until a comparatively recent period, we had nothing that could be called a really decent system of municipal government in the greater part of London. We had, of course, the Lord Mayor and the municipality of the City of London, but then the City of London is only a very small patch in the great metropolis that holds more than five millions of people. London, outside the City, was governed by the old-fashioned parish vestries, and to some extent by a more recent institution which was called the Metropolitan Board of Works. Now, the Metropolitan Board of Works did not manage its affairs very well. There were disagreeable rumors and stories about contracts and jobbing and that sort of thing, and although matters were never supposed to have been quite so bad as they were in New York during days which I can remember well, the days of Boss Tweed, there was enough of public complaint to induce Parliament, at the instigation of Lord Randolph Churchill, to abolish the Board of Works altogether and set up the London County Council, a thoroughly representative body elected by popular suffrage and responsible to its constituents and the public. Lord Rosebery threw himself heart and soul into the promotion of this better system of London municipal government. He became a member of the London County Council, was elected its first Chairman, and later on was re-elected to the same office. Now, I think it would be hardly possible for a man of Lord Rosebery's rank and culture and tastes to give a more genuine proof of patriotic public spirit than he did when he threw himself heart and soul into the work of a municipal council.

Up to that time the business of a London municipality had been regarded as something belonging entirely to the middle class or the lower middle class, something with which peers and nobles could not possibly be expected to have anything to do. A London Alderman had been from time out of mind a sort of figure of fun, a vulgar, fussy kind of person, who bedizened himself in gaudy robes on festive occasions, and was noted for his love of the turtle in quite a different sense from that which Byron gives to the words. Lord Rosebery set himself steadily to the work of London municipal government at a most critical period in its history; his example was followed by men of rank and culture, and some of the most intellectual men of our day have been elected Aldermen of the London County Council. Only think of Frederic Harrison, the celebrated Positivist philosopher, the man of exquisite culture and refinement, the man of almost fastidious ways, the scholar and the writer, becoming an Alderman of the London County Council, and devoting himself to the duties of his position! Lord Rosebery undoubtedly has the honor of having done more than any other Englishman to raise the municipal government of London to that position which it ought to have in the public life of the State.

All that time Lord Rosebery was not neglecting any of the other functions and occupations which had been imposed upon him, or which he had voluntarily taken upon himself. He held the office of First Commissioner of Works in one of Mr. Gladstone's administrations, an office involving the care of all the State buildings and monuments and parks of the metropolis. He was always to be seen at the private views of the Royal Academy and the other great picture galleries of the London season. He was always starting some new movement for the improvement of the breed of horses, and, indeed, there is a certain section of our community among whom Lord Rosebery is regarded, not as a statesman, or a London County Councilor, or a lover of literature, but simply and altogether as a patron of the turf. Meanwhile we were hearing of him every now and then as an adventurous yachtsman, and as the orator of some great commemoration day when a statue was unveiled to a Burke or a Burns.

A more delightful host than Lord Rosebery it would not be possible to meet or even to imagine. I have had the honor of enjoying his hospitality at Dalmeny and in his London home, and I shall only say that those were occasions which I may describe, in the words Carlyle employed with a less gladsome significance, as not easily to be forgotten in this world. No man can command a greater variety of topics of conversation. Politics, travel, art, letters, the life of great cities, the growth of commerce, the tendencies of civilizations, the art of living, the philosophy of life, the way to enjoy life, the various characteristics of foreign capitals—on all such topics Lord Rosebery can speak with the clearness of one who knows his subject and the vivacity of one who can put his thoughts into the most expressive words. I suppose there must be some eminent authors with whose works Lord Rosebery is not familiar, but I can only say that if there be any such, I have not yet discovered who they are—and I have spent a good deal of my time in reading. I have seen Lord Rosebery in companies where painters and sculptors and the writers of books and the writers of plays formed the majority, where political subjects were not touched upon, and I have observed that Lord Rosebery could hold his own with each practitioner of art on the artist's special subject. Lord Rosebery does not profess to be a bookworm or a great scholar, but I do not know any man better acquainted with general literature. Such a man must surely have got out of life all the best that it has to give.

Yet it is certain that the eyes of expectation are still turned upon Lord Rosebery. There is a general conviction that he has something yet to do—that, in fact, he has not yet given his measure. He has been Prime Minister, and he has been leader of the English Liberal party, but in neither case had he a chance of proving his strength. When Mr. Gladstone made up his mind to retire finally from political life, the Queen sent for Lord Rosebery and invited him to form an administration. Now, it is no secret that at that time there were men in the Liberal party whose friends and admirers believed that their length of service gave them a precedence of claims over the claims of Lord Rosebery. There were those who thought Sir William Harcourt had won for himself a right to be chosen as the successor to Mr. Gladstone. On the other side—for there was grumbling on both sides—there were members of the Liberal administration who positively declined to continue in office if Sir William Harcourt were made Prime Minister. These men did not object to serve under Sir William Harcourt as leader of the House of Commons, but they objected to his elevation to the supreme place of Prime Minister. Also, there were Liberals of great influence, who, while they had the fullest confidence in Lord Rosebery and were not fanatically devoted to Sir William Harcourt, objected to the idea of having a Prime Minister in the House of Lords, and a Prime Minister, too, who had never sat in the House of Commons. Now, it would be idle to deny that there was some practical reason for this objection. The House of Commons is the field on which political battles are fought and won. The Commander-in-Chief ought always to be within reach. A whole plan of campaign may have to be changed at a quarter of an hour's notice. It must obviously often be highly inconvenient to have a Prime Minister who cannot cross the threshold of the House of Commons in order to get into instant communication with the leading men of his own party who are fighting the battle.

At all events, I am now only concerned to say that these doubts and difficulties and private disputations did arise, and that, although Lord Rosebery did accept the position of Prime Minister, he must have done so with some knowledge of the fact that certain of his colleagues were not quite satisfied with the new conditions. Lord Rosebery had been most successful as Foreign Secretary during each term when he held the office, but it was well known, before Mr. Gladstone's retirement, that there were some questions of foreign policy on which the old leader and the new were not quite of one opinion. In English political life, and I suppose in the political life of every self-governing country, there are seasons of inevitable action and reaction which must be observed and felt, although they cannot always be explained.

To a distant observer the policy of the Liberal party might have seemed just the same after Mr. Gladstone had retired from politics as it was when he was in the front of political life. But just as the policy which sustained him in his early days as Prime Minister was helped by the reaction which had set in against the aggressive policy of Lord Palmerston, so there came, with the close of Gladstone's Parliamentary career, a kind of reaction against his counsel of peace and moderation. Lord Rosebery was believed to have more of what is called the Imperialist spirit in him than had ever guided the policy of his great leader. Certainly some of Mr. Gladstone's former colleagues in the House of Commons appear to have thought so, and there began to be signs of a growing division in the party. Lord Rosebery's Prime Ministership lasted but a short time. The Government sustained one or two Parliamentary discomfitures, and there followed upon these a positive defeat in the nature of a sort of vote of censure carried by a small majority against a department of the administration, on the ground of an alleged insufficiency in some of the supplies of ammunition for military service. Many a Government would have professed to think little of such a defeat, would have treated it only as a mere question of departmental detail, and would have gone on as if nothing had happened. But Lord Rosebery refused to take things so coolly and so carelessly. Probably he was growing tired of his position under the peculiar circumstances. Perhaps he thought the most manly course he could take was to give the constituencies the opportunity of saying whether they were satisfied with his administration or were not. The Government appealed to the country. Parliament was dissolved, and a general election followed. Then was seen the full force of the reaction which had begun to set in against the Gladstone policy of peace, moderation, and justice. The Conservatives came into power by a large majority. Lord Rosebery was now merely the leader of the Liberal party in Opposition. Even this position he did not long retain. Some of the most brilliant speeches he ever made in the House of Lords were made during this time, but somehow people began to think that his heart was not in the leadership, and before long it was made known to the public that he had ceased to be the Liberal Commander-in-Chief.

Everybody, of course, was ready with an explanation as to this sudden act, and perhaps, as sometimes happens in such cases, the less a man really knew about the matter the more prompt he was with his explanation. Two reasons, however, were given by observers who appeared likely to know something of the real facts. One was that Lord Rosebery did not see his way to go as far as some of his colleagues would have gone in arousing the country to decided action against the Ottoman Government because of the manner in which it was allowing its Christian subjects to be treated. The other was that Lord Rosebery was too Imperialistic in spirit for such men as Sir William Harcourt and Mr. John Morley. No one could impugn Lord Rosebery's motives in either case. He might well have thought that too forward a movement against Turkey might only bring on a great European war or leave England isolated to carry out her policy at her own risk, and in the other case he may have thought that the policy bequeathed by Mr. Gladstone was tending to weaken the supremacy of England in South Africa.

Lord Rosebery then ceased to lead a Government or a party, and became for the time merely a member of the House of Lords. I do not suppose his leisure hung very heavy on his hands. I cannot imagine Lord Rosebery finding any difficulty in passing his day. The only difficulty I should think such a man must have is how to find time to give a fair chance to all the pursuits that are dear to him. Lord Rosebery spent some part of his leisure in yachting, gave his usual attention to the turf, was to be seen at picture galleries, and occasionally addressed great public meetings on important questions, and was a frequent visitor to the House of Commons during each session of Parliament. The peers have a space in the galleries of the House of Commons set apart for their own convenience, and, although that space can hold but a small number of the peers, yet on ordinary nights its benches are seldom fully occupied. But when some great debate is coming on, then the peers make a rush for the gallery space in the House of Commons, and those who do not arrive in time to get a seat have to wait and take their chance, each in his turn, of any vacancy which may possibly occur. I am not a great admirer of the House of Lords as a legislative institution, and I must say that it has sometimes soothed the rancor of my jealous feelings as a humble Commoner to see a string of peers extending across the lobby of the House of Commons, each waiting for his chance of filling some sudden vacancy in the peers' gallery.

Lord Rosebery continued to attend the debates when he had ceased to be Prime Minister and leader of the Liberal party just as he had done before. His fine, clearly cut, closely shaven face, with features that a lady novelist of a past age would have called chiseled, and eyes lighted with an animation that seemed to have perpetual youth in it, were often objects of deep interest to the members of the House, and to the visitors in the strangers' galleries, and no doubt in the ladies' gallery as well. The appearance of Lord Rosebery in the peers' gallery was sure to excite some talk among the members of the House of Commons on the green benches below. We were always ready to indulge in expectation and conjecture as to what Lord Rosebery was likely to do next, for there seemed to be a general consent of opinion that he was the last man in the world who could sit down and do nothing. But what was there left for him to do? He had held various administrative offices: he had twice been Foreign Secretary; he had twice been Chairman of the London County Council; he had been Prime Minister; he had been leader of the Liberal party; he had been President of all manner of great institutions; he had been President of the Social Science Congress; he had been Lord Rector of two great Universities; he had twice won the Derby. What was there left for him to do which human ambition in our times and in the dominions of Queen Victoria could care to accomplish? Yet the general impression seemed to be that Lord Rosebery had not yet done his appointed work, and that impression has grown deeper and stronger with recent events.

Since the day when Lord Rosebery withdrew from the leadership of the Liberal party the division in that party has been growing wider and deeper. The war in South Africa has done much to broaden the gulf of separation. Lord Rosebery is an Imperialist, Sir William Harcourt and Mr. John Morley are not Imperialists. The opponents of Sir William Harcourt and Mr. Morley call them Little Englanders. The opponents of Lord Rosebery and those who think with him would no doubt call them Jingoes. The Imperialist, or, as his opponents prefer to call him, the Jingo, accepts as the ruling principle of his faith the right and the duty of England to spread her civilization and her supremacy as far as she can over all those parts of the world which are still lying in disorganization and in darkness. The Little Englander, as his opponents delight to describe him, believes that England's noblest work for a long time to come will be found in the endeavor to spread peace, education, and happiness among the peoples who already acknowledge her supremacy. I am not going to enter into any argument as to the relative claims of the two political schools. It has been said that a man is born either of the school of Aristotle or of the school of Plato. Perhaps an Englishman of modern times is born a Jingo or a Little Englander. I am not an Englishman, and therefore am not called upon to rank myself on either side of the controversy, but I know full well which way my instincts and sympathies would lead me if I were compelled to choose. I could not, therefore, account myself a political follower of Lord Rosebery; and, indeed, on the one great question which concerned me most as a member of the House of Commons, that of Irish Home Rule, Lord Rosebery is not quite so emphatic as I should wish him to be. I am therefore writing the eulogy, not of Lord Rosebery the politician, but of Lord Rosebery the orator, the scholar, the man of letters and arts and varied culture, the man who has done so much for public life in so many ways, the helpful, kindly, generous friend.

The common impression everywhere is that the Conservative Government, as it is now constituted, cannot last very long. The sands of the present Parliament are running out; the next general election may be postponed for some time yet, but it cannot be very far off. Are the Liberals to come back to power with Lord Rosebery at their head? Can the Liberal party become so thoroughly reunited again, Jingoes and Little Englanders, as to make the formation of a Liberal Government a possible event so soon? Or is it possible, as many observers believe, that Lord Rosebery may find himself at the head of an administration composed of Imperialist Liberals and the more enlightened and generally respected members of the present Government? I shall not venture upon any prediction, having seen the unexpected too often happen in politics to have much faith in political prophecy. I note it as an evidence of the position Lord Rosebery has won for himself that, although he became Prime Minister only to be defeated, and leader of the Liberal party only to resign, he is still one of the public men in England about whom people are asking each other whether the time for him to take his real position has not come at last.

Photograph copyright by Elliott & Fry
**JOSEPH CHAMBERLAIN**

# JOSEPH CHAMBERLAIN

Mr. Chamberlain was once described by an unfriendly critic as the Rabagas of English political life. We all remember Rabagas, the hero of Sardou's masterpiece of dramatic satire, who begins his public career and wins fame among certain classes as a leveler and a demagogue of the most advanced views, an unsparing enemy of the aristocracy, a man who will make no terms with the privileged orders, and will bow to no sovereign but the sovereign people. Now, I have said that it was an unfriendly critic who likened Mr. Chamberlain to Sardou's creation, but it was not in the earlier career of the real or the imaginary politician that the resemblance was especially to be traced. Rabagas is brought by tempting conditions under the influence of the privileged classes, the aristocracy, and the reigning sovereign of the small state in which he lives; and his leveling and revolutionary tendencies melt away under the genial influence of his new associations. He becomes, before long, the admirer of the aristocracy and the Prime Minister of the Prince, and is ready to devote all his energies to the defense of the privileged orders, to the repression of the vile democracy, and the silencing of Radical orators.

In this contrast between the earlier and the later parts of the political career the malevolent critic, no doubt, found the materials for his comparison between Rabagas and Mr. Chamberlain. For there can be no denying that Mr. Chamberlain began his public life as an eloquent, an unsparing, and apparently a convinced champion of democracy against the aristocracy, the privileged orders, and the Conservative party, and that he is now a leading member of a Conservative Government, and goes further than most of his colleagues would be likely to go in his hostility to Radical measures and to Radical men.

Moreover, Mr. Chamberlain, who during the earlier part of his public life belonged to the party most strenuously opposed to all unnecessary wars, and especially wars which had annexation for their object, has been the chief Ministerial promoter of the late war in South Africa, a war which had for its object the subjugation of two independent republics in order to bring them under the Imperial flag of England. No one, therefore, could have been much surprised when the unfriendly critic fancied that he could discover at least a certain superficial resemblance between the career of Rabagas and the career of Mr. Chamberlain.

I have been a close observer of much of Mr. Chamberlain's public life, and for some time we were thrown a good deal into Parliamentary and political association. He came into the House of Commons not very long before I had the honor of obtaining a seat there, and his fame had preceded him so far that his entrance into Parliament was looked upon by everybody as a coming event, in the days when he had not yet been elected to represent the constituency of Birmingham. Birmingham was at that time one of the most thoroughly Radical cities in England. John Bright once said that as the sea, wherever you dip a cup into it, will be found to be salt, so the constituency of Birmingham, wherever you test it, will be found to be Radical. Birmingham could claim the merit of being one of the best organized municipalities in England. Its popular educational institutions were excellent; its free libraries might have won the admiration of a citizen of Boston, Massachusetts; its police arrangements were efficient; its sanitation might well have been the envy of London, and the general intelligence of its citizens was of the highest order. Now, it was in this enlightened, progressive, and capable community that Mr. Chamberlain won his first fame. He is not a Birmingham man by birth. He was, I believe, born and brought up on the south side of London, and was educated at University College School, London. But at an early age he settled in Birmingham, and became a member of his father's manufacturing firm there. Very soon he rose to great distinction as a public speaker and as a member of the local corporation, and three times was elected chief magistrate of Birmingham. We began soon to hear a great deal of him in London. It must have been clear to anybody who knew anything of Birmingham that a man could not have risen to such distinction in that city without great intelligence and a marked capacity for public life. All this time he was known as a Radical of the Radicals. The Liberal party in London began to look upon him as a coming man, and as a coming man who was certain to take his place, and that probably a leading place, in the advanced Radical division of the Liberals. His political speeches showed him to be a democrat of the leveling order—a democrat, that is to say, of views much more extreme than had ever been professed by John Bright or Richard Cobden. He was an unsparing assailant of the aristocracy and the privileged classes, and, indeed, went so far in his Radicalism that the Conservatives in general regarded him as a downright Republican.

I can well remember the sensation which his first speech in the House of Commons created among the ranks of the Tories after his election to Parliament as one of the representatives of Birmingham. The good Tories made no effort to conceal their astonishment at the difference between the real Chamberlain as they saw and heard him and the Chamberlain of their earlier imaginings. I talked with many of them at the time, and was made acquainted with their emotions. Judging from his political speeches, they had set him down as a wild Republican, and they expected to see a rough and shaggy man, dressed with an uncouth disregard for the ways of society, a sort of Birmingham Orson who would probably scowl fiercely at his opponents in the House and would deliver his opinions in tones of thunder. The man who rose to address the House was a pale, slender, delicate looking, and closely shaven personage, very neatly dressed, with short and carefully brushed hair, and wearing a dainty eyeglass constantly fixed in his eye. "He looks like a ladies' doctor," one stout Tory murmured. "Seems like the model of a head clerk at a West End draper's," observed another. Certainly there was nothing of the Orson about this well-dressed, well-groomed representative of the Birmingham democracy. Mr. Chamberlain's speech made a distinct impression on the House. It was admirably delivered, in quietly modulated tones, the clear, penetrating voice never rising to the level of declamation, but never failing to reach the ear of every listener. The political opinions which it expressed were such as every one might have expected to come from so resolute a democrat, but the quiet, self-possessed delivery greatly astonished those who had expected to see and hear a mob orator. Mr. Chamberlain's position in the House was assured after that first speech. Even among the Tories everybody felt satisfied that the new man was a man of great ability, gifted with a remarkable capacity for maintaining his views with ingenious and plausible argument, a man who could hold his own in debate with the best, and for whom the clamors of a host of political opponents could have no terrors.

I may say at once that Mr. Chamberlain has, ever since that time, proved himself to be one of the ablest debaters in the House of Commons. He is not and never could be an orator in the higher sense, for he wants altogether that gift of imagination necessary to the composition of an orator, and he has not the culture and the command of ready illustration which sometimes lift men who are not born orators above the mere debater's highest level. But he has unfailing readiness, a wide knowledge of public affairs, a keen eye for all the weak points of an opponent's case, and a flow of clear and easy language which never fails to give expression, at once full and precise, to all that is in his mind. He was soon recognized, even by his extreme political opponents, as one of the ablest men in the House of Commons, and it seemed plain to every one that, when the chance came for the formation of a Liberal Ministry, the country then being in the hands of a Tory Government, Mr. Chamberlain would beyond question find a place on the Treasury Bench.

Meanwhile Mr. Chamberlain's democratic views seemed to have undergone no modification. He was as unsparing as ever in his denunciation of the aristocracy and the privileged classes, and he was especially severe upon the great landowners, and used to propound schemes for buying them out by the State and converting their land into national property. His closest ally and associate in Parliamentary politics was Sir Charles Dilke, who had entered the House of Commons some years before Mr. Chamberlain, and who was then, as he is now, an advanced and determined Radical. Sir Charles Dilke, in fact, was at that time supposed to be something very like a Republican, at least in theory, and he had been exciting great commotion in several parts of the country by his outspoken complaints about the vast sums of money voted every year for the Royal Civil List. It was but natural that Sir Charles Dilke and Mr. Chamberlain should become close associates, and there was a general conviction that the more advanced section of the Liberal party was destined to take the command in Liberal politics.

Outside the range of strictly English politics there was a question arising which threatened to make a new division in the Liberal party. This was the question of Home Rule for Ireland as it presented itself under the leadership of Charles Stewart Parnell. For years the subject of Home Rule had been the occasion, under the leadership of Mr. Butt, of nothing more formidable to the House of Commons than an annual debate and division. Once in every session Mr. Butt brought forward a motion calling for a measure of Home Rule for Ireland, and, after some eloquent speeches made in favor of the motion by Irish members, a few speeches were delivered on the other side by the opponents of Home Rule, Liberals as well as Tories, and then some leading member of the Government went through the form of explaining why the motion could not be accepted. A division was taken, and Mr. Butt's motion was found to have the support of the very small Irish Nationalist party, as it then was, and perhaps half a dozen English or Scotch Radicals; and the whole House of Commons, except for these, declared against Home Rule. About the time, however, of Mr. Chamberlain's entrance on the field of politics a great change had taken place in the conditions of the Home Rule question. Charles Stewart Parnell had become in fact, although not yet in name, the leader of the Irish National party, and Parnell's tactics were very different indeed from those of his nominal leader, Mr. Butt. Butt was a man who had great reverence for old constitutional forms and for the traditions and ways of the House of Commons, and he had faith in the power of mere argument to bring the House some time or other to see the justice of his cause. Parnell was convinced that there was only one way of compelling the House of Commons to pay any serious attention to the Irish demand, and that was by making it clear to the Government and the House that until they had turned their full attention to the Irish national claims, they should not be allowed to turn their attention to any other business whatever. Therefore he introduced that policy of obstruction which has since become historical, and which for a time literally convulsed the House of Commons. Now, I am not going again into the oft-told tale of Home Rule and the obstruction policy, and I touch upon the subject here only because of its direct connection with the career of Mr. Chamberlain. Sir Charles Dilke and Mr. Chamberlain supported Mr. Parnell in most of his assaults upon the Tory Government. It was Parnell's policy to bring forward some motion, during the discussion of the estimates for the army and navy or for the civil service, which should raise some great and important question of controversy connected only in a technical sense with the subject formally before the House, and thus to raise a prolonged debate which had the effect of postponing to an indefinite time the regular movement of business. Thus he succeeded in stopping all the regular work of the House until the particular motion in which he was concerned had been fully discussed and finally settled, one way or the other. It was by action of this kind that he succeeded in prevailing upon the House of Commons to condemn the barbarous system of flogging in the army and the navy, and finally to obtain its abolition. In this latter course he was warmly supported by Mr. Chamberlain and Sir Charles Dilke, and by many other Liberal members.

But it was not only in obstructive motions which concerned the common interests of the country that Parnell obtained the support of Sir Charles Dilke and Mr. Chamberlain. These two men boldly and vigorously maintained him in his policy of obstruction when it only professed to concern itself with Irish national questions. They identified themselves so thoroughly with his Irish policy that it became a familiar joke in the House of Commons to describe Dilke and Chamberlain as the Attorney-General and the Solicitor-General of the Home Rule party. I was then a member of the House, and had been elected Vice-President of the Irish party, Parnell being, of course, the President. Naturally, I was brought closely into association with Mr. Chamberlain, and I had for many years been a personal friend of Sir Charles Dilke. Again and again I heard Mr. Chamberlain express his entire approval of the obstructive policy adopted by Parnell, and declare that that was the only way by which Parnell could compel the House of Commons to give a hearing to the Irish claims. Mr. Chamberlain, indeed, expressed, on more than one occasion, in speeches delivered during a debate in the House, just the same opinion as to Parnell's course which I had heard him utter in private conversation. In one of these speeches I remember well his generous declaration that he was sorry he had not had an opportunity of expressing that opinion to the House of Commons long before. Now, of course, I always thought, and still think, that all this was much to the credit of Mr. Chamberlain's political intelligence, courage, and manly feeling, and I regarded him as one of the truest English friends the Home Rule cause had ever made. I had the opportunity, on more than one occasion, of hearing Dilke and Chamberlain define their respective positions on the subject of Home Rule. Dilke regarded Home Rule as an essential part of a federal system, which he believed to be absolutely necessary to the safety, strength, and prosperity of the British Empire. He would have made it a Federal system, by virtue of which each member of the Imperial organization governed its own domestic affairs in its own way, while the common wishes and interests of the Empire were represented, discussed, and arranged in a central Imperial Parliament. Therefore, even if the Irish people had not been themselves awakened to the necessity for a Home Rule Legislature in Ireland, Dilke would have been in favor of urging on them the advantages of such an arrangement. This, in point of fact, is the system which has made the Canadian and the Australasian provinces what they are at this day, contented, loyal, and prosperous members of the Imperial system. Chamberlain was not so convinced an advocate of the general system of Home Rule as Dilke, but he was always emphatic in his declarations that, if the large majority of the Irish people desired Home Rule, their desire should be granted to them by the Imperial Parliament.

When I first entered the House of Commons, the Conservative party was in office. About a year after, the general election of 1880 came on, almost in the ordinary course of events, and the result of the appeal to the country was that the Liberals came back to power with a large majority. Mr. Gladstone was at the head of the Liberal party, and he became Prime Minister. Everybody assumed that two such prominent Radicals as Dilke and Chamberlain could not be overlooked by the new Prime Minister in his arrangements to form an administration. I think I am entitled to say, as a positive fact, that Dilke and Chamberlain entered into an understanding between themselves that unless one at least of them was offered a place in the Cabinet, neither would accept office of any kind. Of course when a new Government is in process of formation all these arrangements are matters of private discussion and negotiation with the men at the head of affairs; and the result of interchange of ideas in this instance was that Chamberlain became President of the Board of Trade, with a seat in the Cabinet, and Dilke accepted the office of Under-Secretary for Foreign Affairs, without a place in the inner Ministerial circle. This was done, not only with Dilke's cordial consent, but at his express wish, for it was his strong desire that the higher place in the administration should be given to his friend.

Now, at this time Mr. Gladstone was not a convinced Home Ruler. I know that the importance of the question was entering his mind and was absorbing much of his attention. I know that he was earnestly considering the subject, and that his mind was open to conviction; but I know also that he was not yet convinced. Chamberlain, therefore, would apparently have had nothing to gain if he merely desired to conciliate the favor of his leader by still putting himself forward as the friend and the ally of the Home Rule party. But he continued, when in office, to be just as openly our friend as he had been in the days when he was only an ordinary member of the House of Commons. There were times when, owing to the policy of coercion pursued in Ireland by the then Chief Secretary to the Lord-Lieutenant, the relations between the Liberal Government and the Home Rule party were severely strained. We did battle many a time as fiercely against Mr. Gladstone's Government as ever we had done against the Government of his Tory predecessor. Yet Mr. Chamberlain always remained our friend and our adviser, always stood by us whenever he could fairly be expected to do so in public, and always received our confidences in private. When Mr. Parnell and other members of our party were thrown into Dublin prison, Mr. Chamberlain did his best to obtain justice and fair treatment for them and for the Home Rule cause and for the Irish people.

Many American readers will probably have a recollection of what was called the Kilmainham Treaty—the "Treaty" being an arrangement which it was thought might be honorably agreed upon between Mr. Gladstone and the leaders of the Irish party, and by virtue of which an improved system of land-tenure legislation was to be given to Ireland, on the one hand, and every effort was to be made to restore peace to Ireland on the other. I do not intend to go into this old story at any length, my only object being to record the fact that the whole arrangements were conducted between Mr. Chamberlain and Mr. Parnell, and that Chamberlain was still understood to be the friend of Ireland and of Home Rule. These negotiations led to the resignation of office by the late Mr. William Edward Forster, Chief Secretary to the Lord-Lieutenant of Ireland; and then came the important question, Who was likely to be put in Mr. Forster's place? I believe that, as a matter of fact, the place was offered, in the first instance, to Sir Charles Dilke, but was declined by him on the ground that he was not also offered a seat in the Cabinet, and Dilke was convinced that unless he had a seat in the Cabinet he could have no chance of pressing successfully on the Government his policy of Home Rule for Ireland.

Mr. Chamberlain then had reason to believe that the office would be tendered to him, and he was willing to accept it and to do the best he could. I know that he believed that the place was likely to be offered to him and that he was ready to undertake its duties, for he took the very frank and straightforward course of holding a conference with certain Irish Nationalist members to whom he made known his views on the subject. The Irish members whom he consulted understood clearly from him that if he went to Ireland in the capacity of Chief Secretary he would go as a Home Ruler and would expect their co-operation and their assistance. There was no secret about this conference. It was held within the precincts of the House of Commons, and Mr. Chamberlain's action in suggesting and conducting it was entirely becoming and proper under the conditions. For some reason or other, which I at least have never heard satisfactorily explained, the office of Chief Secretary was given, after all, to the late Lord Frederick Cavendish. Then followed the terrible tragedy of the Phoenix Park, Dublin, when Lord Frederick and Mr. Thomas Burke, his official subordinate, were murdered in the open day by a gang of assassins. When the news of this appalling deed reached London, Mr. Parnell and I went at once, and as a matter of course, to consult with Sir Charles Dilke and Mr. Chamberlain as to the steps which ought to be taken in order to vindicate the Irish people from any charge of sympathy with so wanton and so atrocious a crime. We saw both Dilke and Chamberlain and consulted with them, and I can well remember being greatly impressed by the firmness with which Mr. Chamberlain declared that nothing which had happened would prevent him from accepting the office of Chief Secretary in Ireland if the opportunity were offered to him. I go into all this detail with the object of making it clear to the reader that, up to this time, Mr. Chamberlain had the full confidence of the Irish Nationalist party and was understood by them to be in thorough sympathy with them as to Ireland's demand for Home Rule.

Mr. Chamberlain did not, however, become Irish Secretary, but retained his position as President of the Board of Trade, and many foreign troubles began in Egypt and other parts of the world which diverted the attention of Parliament and the public for a while from questions of purely domestic policy. Mr. Gladstone, however, succeeded in carrying through Parliament a sort of new reform bill which reconstructed the constituencies, expanded the electorate, and, in fact, set up in the three countries something approaching nearly to the old Chartist idea of equal electoral division and universal suffrage. The foreign troubles, however, were very serious, the Government lost its popularity, and at last was defeated on one of its financial proposals and resigned office. The Tories came into power for a short time. Mr. Chamberlain stumped the country in his old familiar capacity as a Radical politician of the extreme school, and he started a scheme of policy which was commonly described afterwards as the unauthorized programme, in which he advocated, among other bold reforms, a peasant proprietary throughout the country by the compulsory purchase of land, the effect of which would be to endow every deserving peasant with at least three acres and a cow. The Tories were not able to do anything in office, owing to the combined attacks made upon them by the Radicals and the Irish Home Rulers, and in 1886 another dissolution of Parliament took place and a general election came on. The effect of the latest reform measure introduced by Mr. Gladstone now told irresistibly in Mr. Gladstone's favor, and the newly arranged constituencies sent him back into office and into power. Mr. Chamberlain once again joined Mr. Gladstone's Government, and became President of the Local Government Board.

Then comes a sudden change in the story. The extension of the suffrage gave, for the first time, a large voting power into the hands of the majority of the Irish people, for in Ireland up to that date the right to vote had been enjoyed only by the landlord class and the well-to-do middle class; and the result of the new franchise was that Ireland sent into Parliament an overwhelming number of Home Rule Representatives to follow the leadership of Parnell. Gladstone then became thoroughly satisfied that the vast majority of the Irish people were in favor of Home Rule, and he determined to introduce a measure which should give to Ireland a separate domestic Parliament. Thereupon Mr. Chamberlain suddenly announced that he could not support such a measure of Home Rule, and it presently came out that he could not support any measure of Home Rule. He resigned his place in Mr. Gladstone's Government, and he became from that time not only an opponent of Home Rule but a proclaimed Conservative and anti-Radical. When a Tory Government was formed, after the defeat of Mr. Gladstone's first Home Rule measure, Mr. Chamberlain became a member of the Tory Government, and he is one of the leading members of a Tory Government at this day.

Now, it is for this reason, I suppose, that the unfriendly critic, of whom I have already spoken more than once, thought himself justified in describing Mr. Chamberlain as the Rabagas of English political life. It is, indeed, hard for any of us to understand the meaning of Mr. Chamberlain's sudden change. At the opening of 1886 he was, what he had been during all his previous political life, a flaming democrat and Radical. In the early months of 1886 he was a flaming Tory and anti-Radical. During several years of frequent association with him in the House of Commons I had always known him as an advocate of Home Rule for Ireland, and all of a sudden he exhibited himself as an uncompromising opponent of Home Rule. Many English Liberal members objected to some of the provisions of Mr. Gladstone's first Home Rule Bill, but when these objections were removed in Mr. Gladstone's second Home Rule Bill they returned at once to their places under his leadership. But Mr. Chamberlain would have nothing to do with any manner of Home Rule measure, and when he visited the province of Ulster in the north of Ireland he delighted all the Ulster Orangemen by the fervor of his speeches against Home Rule. Moreover, it may fairly be asked why an English Radical and democrat of extreme views must needs become an advocate of Toryism all along the line simply because he has ceased to be in favor of Home Rule for Ireland. These are questions which I, at least, cannot pretend to answer.

Of course we have in history many instances of conversions as sudden and as complete, about the absolute sincerity of which even the worldly and cynical critic has never ventured a doubt. There was the conversion of Constantine the Great, and there was the sudden change brought about in the feelings and the life of Ignatius of Loyola. But then somehow Mr. Chamberlain does not seem to have impressed on his contemporaries, either before or after his great change, the idea that he was a man cast exactly in the mold of a Constantine or an Ignatius. Only of late years has he been dubbed with the familiar nickname of "Pushful Joe," but he was always set down as a man of personal ambition, determined to make his way well on in the world. We had all made up our minds, somehow, that he would be content to push his fortunes on that side of the political field to which, up to that time, he had proclaimed himself to belong, and it never occurred to us to think of him as the associate of Tory dukes, as a leading member of a Tory Government, and as the champion of Tory principles. Men have in all ages changed their political faith without exciting the world's wonder. Mr. Gladstone began as a Tory, and grew by slow degrees into a Radical. Two or three public men in our own days who began as moderate Liberals have gradually turned into moderate Tories. But Mr. Chamberlain's conversion was not like any of these. It was accomplished with a suddenness that seemed to belong to the days when miracles were yet worked upon the earth. Mr. Chamberlain may well feel proud in the consciousness that the close attention of the political world will follow with eager curiosity his further career.

*Photograph copyright by Elliott & Fry*

**HENRY LABOUCHERE**

# HENRY LABOUCHERE

Henry Labouchere is the most amusing speaker in the House of Commons. Eclipse is first and there is no second—to adopt the words once used by Lord Macaulay—at least, if there be a second, I do not feel myself qualified for the task of designating him. It is hardly necessary to say that whenever Labouchere rises in the House of Commons—and he rises very often in the course of a session—he is sure of an immediate hearing. He seldom addresses himself to any subject with the outward appearance of seriousness. He always puts his argument in jesting form; sends a shower of sparkling words over the most solemn controversy; puts on the manner of one who has plunged into the debate only for the mere fun of the thing; and brings his display to an end just at the time when the House hopes that he is only beginning to exert himself for its amusement. I do not know that he has ever made what could be called a long speech, and I think I may fairly assume that he has never made a speech which his audience would not have wished to be a little longer.

Now, I must say at once that it would be the most complete misappreciation of Henry Labouchere's character and purpose to regard him as a mere jester, or even a mere humorist endowed with the faculty of uttering spontaneous witticisms. Labouchere is very much in earnest even when he makes a joke, and his sharpest cynicism is inspired by a love of justice and a desire to champion the cause of what he believes to be the right. I heard him once make a speech in the House of Commons on behalf of some suffering class or cause, and when coming to a close he suddenly said: "I may be told that this is a sentimental view of the case; but, Mr. Speaker, I am a man of sentiment." The House broke into a perfect chorus of laughter at the idea thus presented of Labouchere as a man of sentiment. Probably many, or most, of his listeners thought it was only Labouchere's fun, and merely another illustration of his love for droll paradox. I have no doubt that Labouchere knew very well in advance what sort of reception was likely to be given to his description of himself, and that he heartily enjoyed the effect it produced. But, all the same, there was a good deal of truth in the description. I have always regarded Labouchere as a man of intensely strong opinions, whose peculiar humor it is to maintain these opinions by sarcasm and witticism and seeming paradox.

Certainly no public man in England has given clearer evidence of his sincerity and disinterestedness in any cause that he advocates than Labouchere has done again and again. I remember hearing it said many years ago in New York of my old friend Horace Greeley that whereas some other editors of great newspapers backed up their money with their opinions, Greeley backed up his opinions with his money. The meaning, of course, was that while some editors shaped their opinions in order to make their journals profitable, Horace Greeley was ready to sacrifice his money for the sake of maintaining the newspaper which expressed his sincere convictions. Something of the same kind might fairly be said of Henry Labouchere. He is the proprietor and editor of the weekly newspaper "Truth," in which he expresses his own opinions without the slightest regard for the commercial interests of the paper, or, indeed, for the political interests of the party which he usually supports in the House of Commons. I believe that, as a matter of fact, "Truth" is a most successful enterprise, even as a commercial speculation, for everybody wants to know what it is likely to say on this or that new and exciting question, and nobody can tell in advance what view Labouchere's organ may be likely to take. Labouchere has, however, given proof many times that he keeps up his newspaper as the organ of his individual opinions, and not merely as a means of making money or sustaining the interests of a political party. He has again and again hunted out and hunted down evil systems of various kinds, shams and quacks of many orders, abuses affecting large masses of the poor and the lowly, and has rendered himself liable to all manner of legal actions for the recovery of damages. If, because of some technical or other failure in his defense to one of those legal actions, Labouchere is cast in heavy damages, he pays the amount, makes a jest or two about it, and goes to work at the collection of better evidence and at the hunting out of other shams with as cheery a countenance as if nothing particular had happened. Fortunately for himself, and, I think, also very fortunately for the public in general, Labouchere is personally a rich man, and is able to meet without inconvenience any loss which may be brought upon him now and then by his resolute endeavors to expose shams.

Labouchere spent ten years of his earlier manhood in the diplomatic service, and was attaché at various foreign courts and at Washington. He had always a turn for active political life, and entered the House of Commons in 1865, and in 1880 was elected as one of the representatives for the constituency of Northampton. His colleague at that time in the representation of the constituency was the once famous Charles Bradlaugh. It would not be easy to find a greater contrast in appearance and manners, in education and social bringing up, than that presented by the two representatives of Northampton. Labouchere is a man of barely medium stature; Bradlaugh's proportions approached almost to the gigantic. One could not talk for five minutes with Labouchere and fail to know, even if they had never met before, that Labouchere was a man born and trained to the ways of what is called good society; Bradlaugh was evidently a child of the people, who had led a hard and roughening life, and had had to make his way by sheer toil and unceasing exertion. Bradlaugh as a public speaker was powerful and commanding in his peculiar style—the style of the workingman's platform and of the open-air meetings in Hyde Park. He had tremendous lungs, a voice of surprising power and volume, and his speeches were all attuned to the tone of open-air declamation. Most observers, even among those who thoroughly recognized his great intellectual power and his command of language, would have taken it for granted beforehand that he never could suit himself to the atmosphere of the House of Commons. Labouchere's speeches, even when delivered to a large public meeting, were pitched in a conversational key, and he never attempted a declamatory flight.

His speeches within the House of Commons and outside it always sparkled with droll and humorous illustrations, and when he was most in earnest he seemed to be making a joke of the whole business. Bradlaugh was always terribly in earnest, and seemed as if he were determined to bear down all opposition by the power of his arguments and the volume of his voice. In Labouchere you always found the man accustomed to the polished ways of diplomatic circles; in Bradlaugh one saw the typical champion of the oppressed working class. Labouchere comes, as his name would suggest, from a French Huguenot family of old standing; Bradlaugh was thoroughly British in style even when he advocated opinions utterly opposed to those of the average Briton.

The House of Commons is, on the whole, a fair-minded assembly, and even those who were most uncompromising in their hostility to some of Bradlaugh's views came soon to recognize that by his election to Parliament the House had obtained a new and powerful debater. Both men soon won recognition from the House for their very different characteristics as debaters, and at one time I think that the college-bred country gentlemen of the Tory ranks were inclined, on the whole, to find more fault with Labouchere than with Bradlaugh. They seemed willing to make allowances for Bradlaugh which they would not make for his colleague in the representation of Northampton. One can imagine their reasoning out the matter somewhat in this way: This man Bradlaugh comes from the working class, is not in any sense belonging to our order, and we must take all that into account; while this other man, Labouchere, is of our own class, has had his education at Eton, has been trained among diplomatists in foreign courts, is in fact a gentleman, and yet is constantly proclaiming his hostility to all the established institutions of his native country. Even the Tory country gentlemen, however, found it impossible wholly to resist the wit, the sarcasms, and the droll humors of Labouchere, and whenever he spoke in the House he was sure to have attentive listeners on all the rows of benches.

Bradlaugh's actual Parliamentary career did not last very long. When he was first elected for Northampton, he refused to take the oath of allegiance, on the ground that he could not truthfully make that appeal to the higher power with which the oath concludes. He was willing to make an affirmation, but the majority of the House would not accept the compromise. A considerable period of struggle intervened. The seat was declared to be vacant, but Mr. Bradlaugh was promptly re-elected by the constituents of Northampton, and then there set in a dispute between the House and the constituency something like that which, in the days of Daniel O'Connell, ended in Catholic emancipation. Bradlaugh was enabled to enter the House in 1886, and he made himself very conspicuous in debate. His manners were remarkably courteous, and he became popular after a while even among those who held his political and religious opinions in the utmost abhorrence. His career was closed in 1891 by death.

I can well remember my first meeting with Henry Labouchere. It was at a dinner party given by my friend Sir John R. Robinson, then and until quite lately manager of the London "Daily News." The dinner was given at the Reform Club, and took place, I think, some time before Labouchere's election for Northampton.

I had never seen Labouchere before that time, and had somehow failed to learn his name before we sat down to dinner. We were not a large party, and the conversation was general. I was soon impressed by the vivid and unstrained humor of Labouchere's talk and by the peculiarity of his manner. He spoke his sentences in quiet, slow, and even languid tones; there was nothing whatever of the "agreeable rattle" in his demeanor; he had no appearance of any determination to be amusing, or even consciousness of any power to amuse. He always spoke without effort and with the air of one who would just as soon have remained silent if he did not happen to have something to say, and whatever he did say in his languorous tones was sure to hold the attention and to delight the humorous faculties of every listener. My curiosity was quickly aroused and promptly satisfied as to the identity of this delightful talker, and thus began my acquaintanceship with Labouchere, which has lasted ever since, and is, I hope, likely to last for some time longer. Labouchere is a wonderful teller of stories drawn from his various experiences in many parts of the world, and, unlike most other story-tellers, he is never heard to repeat an anecdote, unless when he was especially invited to do so for the benefit of some one who had not had an opportunity of hearing it before. If he were only a teller of good stories and an utterer of witty sayings, he would well deserve a place in the social history of England during our times; but Labouchere's skill as a talker is one of his least considerable claims upon public attention. Nature endowed Labouchere with what might be called a fighting spirit, and I believe that whenever he sees any particular cause or body of men apparently put under conditions of disadvantage, his first instinctive inclination is to make himself its advocate, so far at least as to insist that the cause or the men must have a fair hearing.

In the House of Commons it could not have happened very often that Henry Labouchere was found on the side of the strong battalions. I know that during the heaviest and the fiercest struggles of the Irish National party against coercive laws and in favor of Ireland's demand for Home Rule, Henry Labouchere was always found voting with us in the division lobby. Some of those days were very dark indeed. Before Gladstone had become converted to the principle of Home Rule for Ireland, and before the later changes in the system of Parliamentary representation had given an extended popular suffrage to the Irish constituencies, the number of Irish representatives who followed the leadership of Charles Stewart Parnell was for many sessions not more than seven or eight. There were some English members who always voted with us, and conspicuous and constant among these were Sir Wilfred Lawson and Henry Labouchere. Unquestionably neither Labouchere nor Lawson had anything whatever to gain in Parliamentary or worldly sense by identifying himself with our efforts in the House of Commons. As soon as Ireland got her fair share of the popular franchise, Parnell was followed by some eighty or ninety members out of the hundred and three who constitute the whole Irish representation. This was the very fact which first brought Gladstone, as I heard from his own lips, to see that the demand of Ireland was in every sense a thoroughly national demand, and that the whole principle of the British constitution claimed for it the consideration of genuine statesmanship. Labouchere had identified himself with the national cause in the days before that cause had yet found anything like representation in the House of Commons. Through all his political career he remained faithful to that principle of nationality, and in the time—I hope not distant—when the Irish claim for Home Rule is recognized and accepted by the British Parliament, Ireland is not likely to forget that Henry Labouchere was one of the very few English members who recognized and championed her claim in the hour when almost every man's hand was against it.

Perhaps the inborn spirit of adventure which makes itself so apparent in Labouchere's temperament and career may have had something to do with his championship of the oppressed. I do not say this with any intention to disparage Labouchere's genuine desire to uphold what he believes to be the right, but only to illustrate the peculiarities of his nature. Certainly his love of adventure has made itself conspicuous and impressive at many stages of his varied career. There is a legend to the effect that Labouchere joined at one time the company of a traveling circus in the United States for the novelty and amusement of the enterprise. I do not know whether there is any truth in this story, but I should certainly be quite prepared to believe it on anything like authentic evidence. The adventure would seem quite in keeping with the temper of the man. Most of us know what happened when the Germans were besieging Paris during the war of 1870. It suddenly occurred to Labouchere that it would be a most interesting chapter in a man's life if he were to spend the winter in the besieged city. No sooner said, or thought, than done. Labouchere was then one of the proprietors of the London "Daily News," and he announced his determination to undertake the task of representing that journal in Paris as long as the siege should last. Of course he obtained full authority for the purpose, and he contrived to make his way into Paris, and when there he relieved the regular correspondent of the "Daily News" from his wearisome and perilous work by sending him off, in a balloon, I believe, to Tours, where he was out of the range of the German forces, and could continue his daily survey of events in general. Then Labouchere set himself down to enjoy all the hardships of the siege, to live on the flesh of horse and donkey and even cat and rat, to endure the setting in of utter darkness when once the sun had gone down, and to chronicle a daily account of his strange experiences. This was accomplished in his "Diary of a Besieged Resident," which appeared from day to day in the columns of the "Daily News," and was afterwards published as a volume, and a most entertaining, humorous, realistic, and delightful volume it made. The very difficulties of its transmission by means of balloons and pigeons and other such floating or flying agencies must have been a constant source of amusement and excitement to the adventurous besieged resident.

Labouchere has always been in the habit of seeking excitement by enterprises on the Stock Exchange. I do not believe that these ventures have been made with the commonplace desire to make money, but I can quite understand that they are prompted by the very same desire for new experiences which prompted the residence in besieged Paris. I remember meeting Labouchere one day many years ago in a West End London street, and being told by him that he had just incurred a very heavy loss by one of his financial ventures on the Stock Exchange. He told me in his usual tones of almost apathetic languor the amount of his loss, and it seemed to my modest experiences in money affairs to be a positive fortune sacrificed. He was smiling blandly while recounting his adventure, and I could not help asking him how he had felt when the loss was first made known to him. "Well," he replied, in the same good-humored tone, "it was an experience, like another." That, I think, is a fair illustration of Labouchere's governing mood. The great thing was to get a new sensation. At one time Labouchere became the founder and the owner of a new theater in London, and he took part in many a newspaper enterprise. He was, as I have said, for a long time one of the proprietors of the "Daily News," and he entered into that proprietorship at the very time when the "Daily News" was making itself most unpopular in capitalist circles and in what is known as society, by its resolute and manly adherence to the side of the Federal States during the great American Civil War. It suited Labouchere's pluck and temper to join in such an undertaking at the time when the odds seemed all against it; and it is only fair to say that I am sure no love for a new sensation could induce Labouchere to take up any cause which he did not believe to be the cause of right.

Labouchere was one of those who went in with the late Edmund Yates in founding "The World," then quite a new venture as a society journal. Labouchere, however, did not long remain a sharer in this enterprise. Yates was the editor of the paper, and Yates went in altogether for satirical or at least amusing pictures of West End life, and did not care anything about politics and the struggles of this or that political movement. Labouchere could not settle down to any interest in a newspaper which dealt only with changes of fashion and the whimsicalities of social life. His close interest in political questions filled him with the resolve to start a journal which, while dealing with the personages and the ways of society, should also be the organ of his own views on graver subjects. He therefore withdrew from all concern in Edmund Yates's "World" and started his own weekly newspaper, "Truth," which has since enjoyed a life of vigor and success. There is room enough for both papers apparently. The "World" has not lost its circle of readers, while "Truth" is beyond question a great power in political and financial as well as in social movements.

One of Labouchere's special delights is to expose in "Truth" some successful adventurer in pretentious financial schemes, some hypocritical projector of sham philanthropic institutions, some charlatan with whom, because of his temporary influence and success, most other people are unwilling to try conclusions. Such an impostor is just the sort of man whom Labouchere is delighted to encounter. Labouchere's plan is simple and straightforward. He publishes an article in "Truth" containing the most direct and explicit charges of imposture and fraud against the man whom he has determined to expose, and he invites this man to bring an action against him in a court of law and obtain damages, if he can, for slander. Labouchere usually intimates politely that he will not avail himself of any preliminary and technical forms which might interpose unnecessary delay, and that he will do all in his power as defendant to facilitate and hasten the trial of the action. It happens in many or most cases that the personage thus invited to appeal to a court of law cautiously refrains from accepting the invitation. He knows that Labouchere has plenty of money, perceives that he is not to be frightened out of his allegations, and probably thinks the safest course is to treat "Truth" and its owner with silent contempt. Sometimes, however, the accused man accepts battle in a court of law, and the attention of the public is riveted on the hearing of the case. Perhaps Labouchere fails to make out every one of his charges, and then the result is formally against him and he may be cast in damages, but he cares nothing for the cost and is probably well satisfied with the knowledge that he has directed the full criticism of the public to the general character of his opponent's doings and has made it impossible for the opponent to work much harm in the future. Even the strongest political antagonists of Labouchere have been found ready to admit that he has rendered much service to the public by his resolute efforts to expose shams and quackeries of various kinds at whatever pecuniary risk or cost to himself.

I do not know whether it would be quite consistent with the realities of the situation if I were to describe Labouchere as a favorite in the House of Commons. He has provoked so many enmities, he has made so many enemies by his sharp sarcasms, his unsparing ridicule, and his sometimes rather heedless personalities, that a great many members of the House must be kept in a state of chronic indignation towards him. A man who arouses a feeling of this kind and keeps it alive among a considerable number of his brother members could hardly be described with strict justice as a favorite in the House of Commons. Yet it is quite certain that there is no man in the House whose sayings are listened to with a keener interest, and whose presence would be more generally missed if he were to retire from public life.

One of the many stories which I have heard about Labouchere's peculiar ways when he was in the diplomatic service is worth repeating here. It has never been contradicted, so far as I know. When Labouchere was attaché to the British Legation at Washington—it was then only a Legation—his room was invaded one day by an indignant John Bull, fresh from England, who had some grievance to bring under the notice of the British Minister. That eminent personage was not then in the house, and the man with the grievance was shown into Labouchere's room. Labouchere was smoking a cigarette, according to his custom, and he received the visitor blandly, but without any effusive welcome. John Bull declared that he must see the Minister at once, and Labouchere mildly responded that the British Minister was not in the Legation buildings. "When will he return?" was the next demand, to which Labouchere could only make answer that he really did not know. "Then," declared the resolute British citizen, "I have only to say that I shall wait here until he returns." Labouchere signified his full concurrence with this proposal, and graciously invited his countryman to take a chair, and then went on with his reading and noting of letters and his cigarette just as before. Hours glided away, and no further word was exchanged. At last the hour came for closing the official rooms, and Labouchere began to put on his coat and make preparations for a speedy departure. The visitor thereupon saw that the time had come for some decided movement on his part, and he sternly put to Labouchere the question, "Can you tell me where the British Minister is just now?" Labouchere replied, with his usual unruffled composure, "I really cannot tell you exactly where he is just now, but I should think he must be nearly halfway across the Atlantic, as he left

New York for England last Saturday." Up rose John Bull in fierce indignation, and exclaimed, "You never told me that he had left for England." "You never asked me the question," Labouchere made answer, with undisturbed urbanity, and the visitor had nothing for it but to go off in storm.

Labouchere is the possessor of a beautiful and historic residence on the banks of the Thames—Pope's famous villa at Twickenham. There he is in the habit of entertaining his friends during the summer months, and there one is sure to meet an interesting and amusing company. I have had the pleasure of being his guest many times, and I need hardly say that I have always found such visits delightful. Labouchere is a most charming host, and although he is himself a wonderful talker, full of anecdote and reminiscence, he never fails to see that the conversation is thoroughly diffused, and that no guest is left out of the talk. In London he always mixes freely with society, and his London home is ever hospitable. Many of his friends were strongly of opinion that he ought to have been invited to become a member of a Liberal administration. I suppose, however, that most of the solid and steady personages who form a Cabinet would have been rather alarmed at the idea of so daring and damaging a free lance being appointed to a high place in the official ranks of a Government, and it would have been out of the question to think of offering any subordinate position to so brilliant a master of Parliamentary debate. For myself I do not feel any regret that Labouchere, so far, has not taken any place in an administration. He has made his fame as a free lance, and has done efficient public work in that capacity, such as he could hardly have accomplished if he had been set down to the regular and routine duties of an official post. He has made a name for himself by his independent support of every cause and movement which he believed to have justice on its side, and I could not think with any satisfaction of a so-called promotion which must submerge his individuality in the measured counsels and compromises of a number of administrative colleagues. I prefer still to think of him as Henry Labouchere, and not as the Right Honorable Gentleman at the head of this, that, or the other department of State.

*Photograph copyright by London Stereoscopic Co.*
**JOHN MORLEY**

# JOHN MORLEY

No English public man of the present day has had a more remarkable political career than that of John Morley. Almost everything that could be against success in political life was against John Morley when he arose from the student's desk to take his place on the political platform. I am not now making any allusion to the difficulties set in a man's way by those accidents which the first Lord Lytton described grandiloquently as the "twin gaolers of the human heart, low birth and iron fortune." I am not quite certain what iron fortune may be, but if I assume it to be early poverty I do not regard it as a very formidable obstruction to human genius in our times. We have many successful men in public life just now who were born in humble station and had to struggle hard for a long time against poverty. John Morley was not born in humble life, as the phrase goes, and had not, so far as I know, to struggle against early poverty. He had an Oxford University education and was called to the bar, but did not make any effort after success in that profession. The difficulties to which I have alluded as standing in his way when he determined to seek a career in political and Parliamentary life had nothing to do with birth and with poverty—they were of quite a different order.

Morley had taken to literature as a profession, and had made for himself a distinguished name as a writer of books and an editor of reviews and newspapers before he obtained a seat in the House of Commons. Now, there is, or used to be, a sort of fixed belief in the British public mind that a literary man is not, in the nature of things, qualified for success in Parliamentary work. We are somewhat getting over this idea of late, and indeed there were at all times living evidences enough to shake such a faith. The generation which recognized the success won in Parliamentary debate by a Macaulay, a Disraeli, and a Bulwer-Lytton might well have got over the notion that literary men cannot succeed in Parliament; but even up to the time of John Morley's election to the House of Commons the idea found still a very general acceptance. Another and much more serious difficulty in John Morley's way was the fact that he was a proclaimed agnostic in questions of religious faith. Now, the average Englishman can hardly be described as one imbued with profound and exalted religious convictions, but it may be taken for granted that he thinks every respectable person who is fit to be a member of Parliament ought to conform to some recognized creed and to attend some authorized place of worship. John Morley was at one time not merely an agnostic, but an avowed and somewhat aggressive agnostic, and his brilliant pen had often been employed to deal satirically with some established doctrine.

In England there is little or no general objection to freedom of opinion so long as it is a question merely of opinion. We may know that a man holds free-thinking opinions, but we feel no wish to inflict any manner of punishment or deprivation on him so long as he keeps his opinions to himself and does not endeavor to make them prevail with others. This, however, was what John Morley had got into the way of doing. When he felt a strong conviction on any subject which seemed to him important, he always endeavored to justify his faith by argument and to bring others round to his views of the question.

I can well remember that many of Morley's admirers and friends were but little gratified when it was first made known that he intended to seek for a seat in the House of Commons. Their impression was that he was just then doing in effective and admirable style the very kind of work for which he was best qualified, and that it was a pity he should run the risk of marring such a career for the sake of entering a political field in which he might possibly win no success, and in which success, even if won, would be poor compensation for the sacrifice of better work. Morley, however, seems to have made up his mind, even at an early period of his career, that he would try his chance in Parliament. So long ago as 1865 he became a candidate for a constituency in the North of England, but was not successful; and in 1880, after he had won genuine celebrity by his biography of Edmund Burke, that of Voltaire, that of Rousseau, and other books of the same order, he became a candidate for the great metropolitan division of Westminster. Here again he was unsuccessful, and it was only in 1883 that he first obtained a seat in the House of Commons as the representative of Newcastle-on-Tyne. I can well remember listening with the deepest interest to his maiden speech in the House of Commons. The general impression of the House was that the speech would prove a failure, for only too many members had already made up their minds, according to the usual fashion of the day, that a successful literary man was not likely to become a Parliamentary success. There was a common impression also that, despite his great gifts as a writer and his proved capacity as a journalist and editor, John Morley must be an impracticable sort of person. He had been at one time well known as an associate of the famous Positivist order of thinkers—the order to which men like Frederic Harrison and Richard Congreve belonged. The average member of Parliament could see no chance for a disciple of that school, which this average member regarded merely as a group of dreamers, to make any mark in a practical assembly where the routine business of legislation had to be carried on. Morley's speech was, however, a distinct and unmistakable success.

What first impressed the House of Commons was the ready, quiet force of Morley's delivery. He had a fine, clear voice, he spoke without notes and without any manifest evidence of preparation, every sentence expressed without effort the precise meaning which he wished to convey, and his style had an eloquence peculiarly its own. What most men expected of him was the philosophical discourse of a student and a thinker no longer in his fitting place, and what was least expected of him was just that which he delivered, a ready, telling, and powerful Parliamentary speech. He had some unexpected difficulties to encounter, because he gave out his opinions so forcibly and so boldly that their utterance called forth frequent interruptions—an unusual event in the case of a maiden speech, which is generally regarded as a mere introductory ceremonial and is taken politely as a necessary matter of form. The House soon found, however, that John Morley's speech did not by any means belong to the ordinary category of maiden performances, and the very interruptions were therefore a positive tribute to the importance of the new member's argument. The interruptions were in every sense fortunate for Morley, because they enabled him at this very first opportunity to prove his ready capacity for debate. He replied on the spur of the moment to every interruption and every interjected question, and he showed all the composure, all the promptitude and the command, of a practiced Parliamentary debater. Every man in the House whose opinion was worth having at once recognized the fact that a new force had come up in Parliamentary debate, and when John Morley resumed his seat he must have known that he had accomplished a complete success. From that time onward John Morley has always been recognized as one of the most powerful speakers in the House of Commons. His voice is clear, resonant, and musical, the light of intellect gleams in his earnest eyes, his argument is always well sustained and set off with varied and appropriate illustration, and whenever he rises to speak he is sure to have a deeply attentive audience.

Morley is not in the highest sense one of the orators of Parliament. He is not to be classed, and has never sought to be classed, with such men as Gladstone and Bright. But, short of the highest gift of eloquence, he has every quality needed to make a great Parliamentary debater. When he addresses the House of Commons, one ceases to think of him merely as the scholar and the author, and he becomes the man who can command the House by the arguments and the eloquence which the House best understands. There are many men of high intellectual capacity who occasionally take part in a Parliamentary debate and who are always regarded as in the House but not of it. John Morley proved from his very first effort that he was of the House as well as in it. I have heard him make great platform speeches, and I think he comes nearer to the highest order of eloquence when addressing an ordinary political meeting than even when addressing the House, but it is quite certain that at the present time the House of Commons has no member who can more completely command its attention. It must be said, too, that the character of the man himself, his transparent sincerity, his absolute devotedness to principle, his fearless and unselfish consistency, count for much in the commanding position which he has obtained. The integrity of Morley's career is absolutely beyond criticism or cavil. It never entered into the mind of his bitterest opponent to suspect for a moment that Morley could be influenced by any personal consideration in the course which he took or the words which he uttered. Other men of high position in Parliament are commonly set down as having taken this or that course, modified or suppressed this or that opinion, for the sake of personal advancement, or at least for the sake of maintaining the interests of a party. But everybody knows that John Morley has never sought for office, and could never be induced to make any compromise of political principle even for the sake of maintaining in power the political party to which he belongs. The universal recognition of that great quality in him has added unspeakably to his influence in Parliament. He was not at any time a frequent speaker in the House of Commons, and of course he never was a mere talker. He speaks only when he has something to say which he believes ought to be said and to be said by him, and he never seems to have any temptation to enter into debate for the mere pleasure of taking part in the controversy. If a man is really a good speaker, the House is always ready to listen to him no matter how often he may speak, for the plain reason that debate has to go on for a certain number of hours each day, and it is more pleasant to listen to a member who talks well than to one who talks badly. But, no matter how effective and eloquent a speaker may be, it is quite certain that the House will give him a more attentive ear if it knows beforehand that whenever he rises to take part in debate it is sure to hear something which up to that moment has not been spoken. John Morley, therefore, very soon became one of that small body of men in the House of Commons whose rising to speak is always regarded as an event of interest and importance.

In the retrospect of John Morley's career one is brought up with something approaching to a shock of surprise when he remembers that at the opening of Morley's Parliamentary life he was closely associated with Joseph Chamberlain. I remember having heard people say at the time that Chamberlain took much credit to himself on the ground that he had urged and prevailed upon John Morley to persevere in seeking a seat in the House of Commons. Mr. Chamberlain was at that time an extreme and uncompromising Radical. He was an avowed and constant supporter of the Home Rule party; was in close alliance with Parnell; took a leading part in the arrangement of the so-called Kilmainham Treaty, and delivered a warm panegyric on Parnell himself and Parnell's policy to a crowded and for the most part an indignant House of Commons. There was, therefore, nothing surprising in the fact that Morley and Chamberlain were at that time friends and allies in political affairs, nor had any one then the faintest reason to believe that Chamberlain was ever destined to undergo a sudden and miraculous conversion to ultra-Tory principles. When Mr. Gladstone came into office in 1886 with what was known to be a Home Rule administration, John Morley obtained the position of Chief Secretary to the Lord-Lieutenant of Ireland, with a seat in the Cabinet. It is not by any means a matter of course that the Irish Chief Secretary should be a Cabinet Minister. Sometimes the Lord-Lieutenant himself has a place in the Cabinet and the Chief Secretary is merely an ordinary member of the Government; sometimes, when the Chief Secretary is regarded as a very strong man, he is invited to a seat in the Cabinet and his official master remains outside. John Morley was recognized from the first by Gladstone as a man of the highest political capacity and character, and when the new administration came to be formed Gladstone made evident this estimate of Morley by offering him a place in the Cabinet. The keenest interest was felt alike both by political friends and political enemies in Morley's management of Irish affairs. The new Secretary for Ireland was entering bravely on an enterprise the immediate success of which was, under the conditions, absolutely impossible. I have no doubt whatever that success could have been easily and completely accomplished if John Morley had been allowed his own way in dealing with the whole Irish question—if, for instance, he had been placed in such a position of dictatorship as that which was given to Lord Durham when Durham was sent out to deal with the rebellion in Canada. Durham saw but one remedy for the long discontents and troubles of the Canadian populations, and that remedy he found in the system of Home Rule which has since made Canada peaceful, prosperous, and well content with the place she holds in the British Empire. If John Morley could have been invested with such powers as those given to Lord Durham, he might have made of Ireland another prosperous and contented Canada. But Morley had to administer the affairs of Ireland at a time when the opinion of the English majority had not yet risen to the principle of Home Rule, at least so far as Ireland was concerned, and without such recognition it was beyond the reach of statesmanship to satisfy the national demands of the Irish people. Every Irish Nationalist knew perfectly well that John Morley's heart and intellect alike were with the cause of Irish Home Rule. All that Morley could do to mitigate the troubles of the country and the people he did bravely and steadfastly. Ireland was then the victim of an accumulation of coercion laws which made almost every popular movement, every attempt to maintain an oppressed tenant against an oppressive landlord, every protest against despotic legislation, liable to be treated as an offense calling for the interference of the police. John Morley did all that could be done to mitigate the rigors of such a system, and to administer Ireland on something like the principles of civilization and freedom. He had in this task the full support, encouragement, and sympathy of the statesman who was then Lord-Lieutenant of Ireland—the Earl of Aberdeen, a man of the most thoroughly Liberal principles and a sincere friend to Ireland. But, of course, neither Lord Aberdeen nor John Morley could abolish at a word of command a whole system of penal legislation, and all that could be done was to take care that the laws should be administered in a temperate and reasonable spirit, and that the rulers of Ireland should show themselves to be at heart the friends of Ireland.

There comes back to my memory a somewhat curious illustration of the difficulties which then stood in the way of any cordial intercourse between the representatives of English rule in Ireland and the representatives of the Irish national cause, and I cannot resist the temptation to tell the story here. During Morley's first term of office as Chief Secretary I made some visits to Dublin. I had many meetings with Morley, of course, and he invited me to dine with him at the Chief Secretary's Lodge in Phoenix Park. Now, there had been during all my time a rigorous rule among Irish Nationalists not to accept any of the hospitalities of those who exercised imperial authority in Dublin. No true Nationalist would make one at any social gathering in the official residence of the Viceroy or the Chief Secretary. There were more than merely sentimental reasons for such a principle. In former days the Irish people had in several well-remembered instances seen some vehement advocate of the Irish National cause won over by the promises and the blandishments of Dublin Castle to take office under the Government and to renounce the political faith the profession of which had won for him his seat in Parliament. Therefore it was above all things necessary, in order to maintain the confidence of the Irish people, that the national representatives should show themselves determined not to be drawn into any familiar social relations with the representatives of English rule in Ireland. This was especially a part of Parnell's policy, and on it Parnell laid much stress. John Morley came over to Ireland in a spirit of full friendship towards the Irish people, and he had every reason to believe that the Irish people thoroughly understood his feelings and his hopes. He and I had known each other during many years in London, and when we met in Dublin, he, being still new to the conditions of the place, invited me to dine with him. I explained to him that, however delighted I should be to dine with my friend John Morley, it was quite impossible that I should dine with the Chief Secretary at his official residence in Dublin. I assured him that if I were to accept such an invitation the Tory papers of Dublin would be certain to make characteristic comments on the fact that the Chief Secretary to the Lord-Lieutenant and the Vice-Chairman of the Irish Parliamentary party had been dining together in the Chief Secretary's official home, and that we should both alike find ourselves the objects of something approaching to a public scandal. Morley was surprised at first and then a good deal amused, but he accepted my explanation, and thoroughly understood that it was not any want of friendly feeling which led me to decline his invitation. So we parted as good friends as ever. We still met frequently and talked over questions relating to Irish administration. One day Morley came to see me at the Shelburne Hotel, which was then my home in Dublin. We had a long talk, and, as the hour was growing late, I asked him to stay and dine with me, not remembering at the time that the eye of the public was supposed to be on our movements. One of Morley's happiest gifts is a delightful sense of humor. He rose to the situation at once. Addressing me in solemn tones, but with a gleam of the comic in his eyes, he informed me that if my principles did not allow me to dine with the Chief Secretary in Dublin, so neither did the Chief Secretary's principles allow him to dine there with me. Thus, as some newspaper writers would say, the incident terminated, and we made no further effort at convivial meetings in Dublin.

John Morley's quick sense of humor is not one of the qualities which a stranger would naturally look for in him. Those who have not met him and have known him only through his writings are apt to think of him as a grave and even an austere man, a man wholly immersed in the serious contemplation of life and history, and, if endowed with any sense of humor, only with a sense of its more grim and saturnine aspects. The man himself is altogether and curiously unlike the impression thus formed of him very commonly by those to whom he is not personally known. John Morley has a quick, keen, and delightful sense of humor. He can talk on any subject from grave to gay, from lively to severe. He is one of the most charming of companions, and he is a great favorite among women, even among those who do not greatly concern themselves with the question of woman's political emancipation. There is nothing of the stern philosopher about his manner of comporting himself in social life. Indeed, for all the clear composure of his philosophic contemplations, he has a temperament far too quick and sensitive to allow of his meeting all life's vexatious questions in the mood of stoical endurance. He is by nature somewhat nervous, is decidedly quick in temper, frankly acknowledges that he is rather impatient of contradiction, and is likely to become overheated in the course of an eager argument. I feel the less hesitation in noticing these little peculiarities on the part of my friend because I have heard Morley himself speak of them with perfect frankness as some of his troubles in political controversy. I must say that, so far as I know, these unphilosophical qualities of Morley's temperament only tend to make him all the more a charming friend to his friends. We may admire the marble-like composure of the stern philosopher who yields to no passing human weaknesses of temper, but it must be very hard to keep always on friendly terms with so superhuman a personage.

Mr. Morley goes into society a good deal in London, is often to be seen at the theaters on first nights, seems to enjoy a dinner party or an evening party as well as the most commonplace among us might do, but I do not believe that he has any liking for great shows and pompous celebrations and the other formal demonstrations of Court festivity and Ministerial display. In his quiet London home he leads the life of a man of culture, a scholar and a writer, so far as his political and Parliamentary engagements allow him leisure for such recreation, and he neither seeks the madding crowd nor shuns it. It has always been a wonder to me how such a man can find time for his many and diverse studies and occupations, and should never either neglect the work of his life or shut himself away from its reasonable enjoyments. John Morley is indeed a rare and almost unique combination of the philosophical thinker, the vivid biographer, the Parliamentary debater, and the practical administrator. His life of Richard Cobden is one of the most complete and characteristic pieces of biography accomplished during our time. There would not seem to have been much that was congenial between the temperament of Richard Cobden and that of John Morley. Cobden was not a laborious student of the past; he had no widespread and varied literary or artistic sympathies; he did not concern himself much with any scientific studies except those which have to do with the actual movements of man's working lifetime; he was a great practical reformer, not a scholar, a philosopher, or even a devoted lover of books. I do not know that John Morley was personally well acquainted with Cobden, and I am rather inclined to believe that in his biography of the great free-trader he relied mainly on Cobden's correspondence and on the information given to him by members of Cobden's family. Yet he has created a perfect living picture of Cobden as Cobden's friends all knew him, and he has shown to coming generations, not merely what Cobden said and did, what great reforms he accomplished, and what further reforms he ever had in view, but he has shown what Cobden actually was, and made the man himself a familiar figure to all who read the book. So far as I can judge, he has achieved the same success when telling us of Burke, of Voltaire, and of Rousseau, and has made us feel that with his guidance we come to know the men themselves as well as the parts they performed in politics or in literature.

Morley has for a long time been engaged in preparing his life of Gladstone, and the mind of England, which has lately been distracted by the vicissitudes of war, is now free to turn to quieter thoughts, and to look with eager expectation for the completion of the book. No other living man could have anything like John Morley's qualifications as the biographer of Gladstone. He is one of the greatest masters of lucid and vigorous English prose. He has been what I may call a professional student of the lives of great men; he is a profound political thinker; and he has the faculty of describing to the life and making his subject live again. In addition to all these claims to the position of Gladstone's authorized biographer comes the fact that Morley was for many years intrusted with Gladstone's fullest confidence. To no one did Gladstone make his feelings and his purposes on all political questions more fully known than to John Morley; and I think I am justified in saying that at more than one critical period in his later political history

Gladstone chose Morley as his especial and, for the time, his only confidant. I can say of my own knowledge that in the later years of Gladstone's active political life there were momentous occasions when John Morley acted as the one sole medium of private communication between Gladstone and the leaders of the Irish party. I know, too, how careful and methodical Morley showed himself on all such occasions, and with what ample and accurate notes he preserved the exact record of every day's intercommunications. This is, indeed, one of Morley's characteristic peculiarities—the combination of exalted thought with the most minute attention to the very routine of practical work. That combination of qualities will display itself, I feel quite certain, with complete success in Morley's history of Gladstone's life. John Morley has still, we may well hope, a long political career before him. When the Liberal party next comes into power, John Morley will unquestionably have one of its most commanding offices placed at his disposal. Meanwhile he has ample work on hand even for his energy and perseverance. He is just finishing his life of Gladstone, and is to take charge of the magnificent library which belonged to the late Lord Acton, the greatest English scholar and book-lover of our time. Mr. Carnegie's gift of this great library, lately bought by him, to John Morley, is an act which does honor to the intellect as well as to the heart of the generous donor. Whatever positions, honors, or responsibilities maybe yet before John Morley, it may be taken for granted that he has already won for himself a secure place in the literature and the political life of his country, and that his name will live in its history.

*Photograph by William Notman & Son*

**THE EARL OF ABERDEEN**

# THE EARL OF ABERDEEN

The Earl of Aberdeen will always be associated in my mind with a most hopeful season of our political life, a season none the less cherished in memory and none the less auspicious because its hopes were doomed to temporary disappointment. That bright season was the time when Mr. Gladstone was endeavoring to carry out his policy of Home Rule for Ireland. I need hardly tell my American readers that Gladstone's policy was condemned to failure, partly because of a secession of Liberals who went over to the Conservative ranks for the purpose of opposing the measure, and then because of the attitude taken by the House of Lords, who, thus encouraged, rejected the bill after it had passed the House of Commons. The season, therefore, which I am now recalling to memory was that which came between Mr. Gladstone's promulgation of his Home Rule policy and the rejection of his second measure of Home Rule. The interval was one full of the brightest hopes for all true British Liberals and all Irish Nationalists. For the first time during my recollection, British Liberalism and Irish Nationalism were in true companionship and concord. We fraternized as English and Irish politicians had probably never fraternized before. On both sides we were filled with the fond belief that the disunion of Great Britain and Ireland was soon to come to an end, and that the true and lasting union of the two peoples would be accomplished by Gladstone's policy of giving to Ireland her national self-government. It was a season of much festivity in London, and the Irish Nationalist members of Parliament were welcome guests in all the great Liberals' houses. No figures are more thoroughly associated in my memory with that time than those of Lord Aberdeen and his gifted and noble-minded wife.

Lord Aberdeen is the grandson of that Earl of Aberdeen whose coalition ministry, a luckless effort at a temporary compromise between hostile political forces, came to a disastrous end during the Crimean War. The present Earl succeeded to the title in 1870. He was educated at the University of St. Andrews, in Scotland, and afterwards at University College, Oxford. Lord Aberdeen was a Conservative in his political principles when he entered the House of Lords. But he had too much intellect and too much independence of mind to remain long in subserviency to the traditional creed of a mere party. He differed from his leaders on several important questions before he had fully seen his way to take up his position as a recognized member of the Liberal organization. Most of us who had followed his career thus far with any attention felt sure that the Conservatives would not long be able to keep such a man among their slow-going and unenlightened ranks, and no surprise was felt on either side when he took his natural place as a follower of Mr. Gladstone. Lord Aberdeen became an earnest advocate of the Home Rule policy, and all the noble influence that he and his wife could bring to bear publicly and privately was exerted in support of the cause. Then it was that I first came to know Lord and Lady Aberdeen. I have before me just now a book called "Notables of Britain," described on its title-page as "An Album of Portraits and Autographs of the Most Eminent Subjects of Her Majesty in the Sixtieth Year of Her Reign." This book was published at the office of the "Review of Reviews," and was understood to be the production of Mr. W. T. Stead. It contains an excellent full-length photograph of Lord Aberdeen, who, I may say, has a face and figure well worthy to be preserved by painter and photographer for the benefit of those who in coming days are interested in the notables of Britain. The portrait, like all the other portraits in the volume, is accompanied by an autograph line or two. Lord Aberdeen's written words seem to me peculiarly characteristic of the writer's bright and hopeful spirit. I quote his words—the writing is clear and well formed:—

> I think this is a good motto:
> "*Transeunt nubes—manet cælum.*"
>
> ABERDEEN.

The temper in which Lord Aberdeen conducted all his political intercourse during this period of promise was one of unchanging courage and hopefulness. He was one of the most active and ready among the supporters of Mr. Gladstone, and he found an untiring and invaluable companion in his charming wife. At that time we used to hold political gatherings in private houses as well as in public halls, and I have taken part in more than one Home Rule demonstration held in the private dwellings of some of Mr. Gladstone's colleagues in office. We used to have many social meetings for the purpose of bringing Englishmen and Irishmen into close association. Even Parnell himself was prevailed upon to abandon for the time his rule of seclusion from society, and to meet Mr. Gladstone and Lord Spencer and other leading Englishmen at private dinner parties. Lord Aberdeen was one of the most conspicuous and one of the most attractive figures in these political and social gatherings, and I could not, indeed, recall that period to memory for a moment without finding his figure photographed prominently in it. It was an interesting sight during all that time to see some of the most extreme and most aggressive members of the Irish Parliamentary party mingling in social life with British peers and magnates who only a few years before would probably have regarded those Irish members as traitors to the Queen and fitting inmates of the prison cell. On the other hand, too, it must be said that only a very few years before the Irish Nationalist member who was known to make his appearance in the London drawing-rooms of English aristocracy would have been set down by the majority of his countrymen as a flunkey in spirit and a traitor to his cause. There was a time not long before when an Irish Nationalist member would have needed some courage to enable him to meet his constituents on election day if the local papers had made it known that he was in the habit of showing himself in the drawing-rooms of English peers. All this sudden and complete change had been brought about by the genius and policy of Gladstone when he came to see the true meaning and the true claims of the demand for Irish Home Rule. My memory goes back with a somewhat melancholy pleasure to those days of hope and confidence when the true union of Great Britain and Ireland seemed actually on the verge of consummation. Nor have I the slightest doubt that the lessons taught during that season will have their full influence once again when the period of reaction is over, and that Gladstone's policy of 1886 will come to life again before very long and will accomplish its work once for all.

In that year, 1886, Gladstone appointed Lord Aberdeen to the office of Lord-Lieutenant of Ireland. The position was given to Lord Aberdeen with the frankly proclaimed purpose that he was to be the Lord-Lieutenant of a Home Rule policy, and, indeed, on no other conditions would Lord Aberdeen have consented to accept the office. Lord Aberdeen's short term of rule in Ireland was a complete success. There was not much that the most Liberal Lord-Lieutenant could do in the way of positive administration for the benefit of the island. There was already in existence a whole code of repressive legislation compiled during successive ages of despotic government, and this existing code it was not in the power of Lord Aberdeen or any other Viceroy to abolish or even to modify. All that the new Lord-Lieutenant could do in the way of political relief to the Irish people was to discourage as much as possible the too frequent application of the coercive laws and to make it known that the sympathies of the new Government were in favor of political freedom for Ireland, as well as for England and Scotland. Lord Aberdeen fulfilled this part of his public duty with a brave heart and with all the success possible to the task. Every one who had any acquaintance with the state of Ireland at the time must have known what difficulties were likely to be set in the way of Lord Aberdeen's endeavor to mitigate the severities of the coercion system. The most serious of those difficulties would in all probability have come from the permanent official staff in Dublin Castle. American readers in general can have but little idea as to the peculiarities of that singular institution Dublin Castle, the center and fortress of Irish government. It has become, from generations of usage, a very bulwark against the progress of Irish national sentiment. The fresh current of feeling from the outside seems to make little impression on its stagnant and moldy atmosphere. It is ruled by tradition, and to that tradition belongs the rule of hostility to every popular feeling and every national demand. Lord Aberdeen had to encounter all the resistance which the dead weight of Dublin Castle's antiquated systems could bring to bear against his liberal and enlightened efforts at the pacification of the country. He carried out his purpose with unflinching resolve and unruffled temper, and, so far as the existing laws allowed him, he mitigated the harshnesses of the system under which Ireland had been governed since the Act of Union. But there was, of course, much more within Lord Aberdeen's capacity to accomplish than the mere mitigation of existing laws which it was not in his power to abolish. His presence and the entire conduct of his viceroyalty were as a proclamation to the Irish people that the whole sympathies of the Gladstone Government went with the national demands.

Then, indeed, a strange sight was to be seen in Dublin—the sight of a thoroughly popular welcome, a national welcome, given to the representative of English rule in Ireland. A new chapter in Irish history seemed to open, and the heart of Ireland was filled with hope. It is told of Swift that when Carteret, Earl Gran-

## THE EARL OF ABERDEEN

ville, was appointed Lord-Lieutenant of Ireland—Swift afterwards became one of Granville's close friends—he exclaimed in his sarcastic fashion that he could not understand why such a man should be appointed to such an office, and he thought the Government ought to keep on sending its bullies and blockheads just as before. A satirical Nationalist might have been expected to break forth into a similar expression of wonder when a man like Lord Aberdeen was sent to Ireland to carry on the rule of Dublin Castle. Lord Aberdeen and his wife made themselves popular everywhere among the Irish people, showed a living and a constant interest in everything that concerned the welfare of the population, and did all they could to break down the long-existing barricades which made England and Ireland hostile nations. When Mr. Gladstone failed in carrying his Home Rule Bill through the House of Commons and his Government came to an end, Lord Aberdeen took his leave of Ireland amid demonstrations of popular regard, affection, and regret which must have deeply touched his generous heart. In 1893, when the Liberals were again in power, Lord Aberdeen was made Governor-General of Canada, and he held that position until 1898. His term of service in Canada was as successful as might have been expected, and the French as well as the other provinces looked up to him with admiration and gratitude. Then, for the time, his official career came to an end. In the interval between the Irish and the Canadian appointment Lord Aberdeen and his wife made a tour round the world, visiting on their way India and most of the British colonies. The name of Lady Aberdeen is associated with all great movements which have to do with the education and the general advancement of women, and with many good works undertaken for the benefit of the Irish peasantry. Lady Aberdeen, it should be said, is the youngest daughter of the first Lord Tweedmouth, and is sister of the Lord Tweedmouth who, as Edward Marjoribanks, was so well known for a long time as one of the leading Whips of the Liberal party. Lady Aberdeen's name is Ishbel Maria, and I may ask my American readers not to make the mistake, sometimes made even in England, of assuming her name to be the more familiar one of Isabel. She has always been one of the most prominent, influential, and graceful figures in English society, and every charitable association which deserves her support has the advantage of her help, her protection, and her guidance. I know from my own experience what valuable and untiring service she has given to the promotion of the lace-making and the cottage industries of Ireland. I had the great honor of being associated with her in some of these efforts, and I never can forget her unsparing devotion to the best interests of every such effort. I have among my books a series of large and handsome volumes devoted to a record of the proceedings which took place at the International Council of Women held in London during July of 1899 and presided over by the Countess of Aberdeen. This series, published by Mr. Fisher Unwin, is edited by Lady Aberdeen and has an introduction written by her. I may quote the closing paragraph of the introduction:—

> It is a great inspiration to be bound together in the pursuance of high ideals; it is also a grave responsibility—and during our recent Council meeting both these thoughts have been made very real to us. I pray God that they may abide within the hearts of all who, in every country, are the guardians of the honor of our

Council, so that it may prove true to the lofty profession it has made.

The series contains seven volumes, every one of which has been carefully edited by Lady Aberdeen, and is enriched with many commentaries of her own. One can easily imagine the amount of time and trouble which such a work must have imposed on a busy woman, and those who know anything of her will know the thought and care and devotion which she must have given to such a labor of love.

Not a few persons are still apt to associate the idea of a woman advocating the advancement of women with something unfeminine, ungracious, self-assertive, and overbearing. When Lady Aberdeen first began to be known in social movements, the memory of the late Mrs. Lynn Linton's diatribes about "the Shrieking Sisterhood" was still fresh in the public mind, and much prejudice yet lingered against the women who publicly devoted themselves to the advancement of their sex. Lady Aberdeen might have seemed as if she were specially created to be a living refutation of all such absurd ideas. No fashionable woman given up to social success and distinction in drawing-rooms, dining-rooms, balls, and Court ceremonials could have been more feminine, graceful, and charming in her ways and her demeanor than this noble-hearted woman, who was not afraid to advocate the genuine rights of women, and who stood by her husband's side in all his efforts for political reform. One might adopt the words which Sheridan has made the opening of a song in "The Duenna," and proclaim that a pair was never seen more justly formed to meet by nature than Lord and Lady Aberdeen. Such an impression was assuredly formed in Ireland and in Canada, and indeed in every place where Lord and Lady Aberdeen were able to assert their unostentatious and most beneficent influence.

Lord Aberdeen succeeded to the title and its responsibilities at too early an age to allow him any opportunity of proving his capacity for Parliamentary life in the House of Commons. His elder brother was drowned on a voyage from Boston to Melbourne, and the subject of this article then became Earl of Aberdeen, with, as a matter of course, a seat in the House of Lords. There is nothing like a real Parliamentary career to be found in the House of Lords. A man of great natural gifts can, of course, give evidence even there that he is born for statesmanship and can command attention by his eloquence. Lord Aberdeen made it certain even in the House of Lords that he was endowed with these rare qualifications. But the House of Lords has no influence over the country, unless, indeed, when it exerts itself to stay for the time the progress of some great and popular measure. Even this is only for the time, and if the measure be really one of national benefit and deserving of public support, it is sure to be carried in the end, and the Lords have to give in and to put up with their defeat. But the hereditary chamber is not even a commanding platform from which an eloquent speaker can address and can influence the whole country, and the temptations there to apathy and indolence must often be found to be almost irresistible. On rare occasions, two or three times in a session, perhaps, there comes off what is popularly called a full-dress debate, and then the red benches of the House, on which the peers have their seats, are sure to be crowded, and the galleries where members of the House of Commons are entitled to sit and the galleries allotted to strangers are also well occupied. The Lords have even the inspiriting advantage, denied to the House of Commons, of open galleries where ladies can sit in the full glare of day or of gaslight, and can encourage an orator by their presence and their attention. In the House of Commons, as everybody knows, the small number of ladies for whom seats are provided are secreted behind a thick grating, and thus become an almost invisible influence, if, indeed, they can hope to be an influence at all. Yet even this inspiration does not stir the peers to anything more than the rarest attempts at a great debate. On ordinary occasions—and these ordinary occasions constitute nearly the whole of a session—the peers sit for only an hour or so every day, and then mutter and mumble through some formal business, and the outer public does not manifest the slightest interest in what they are doing or trying to do. There are many men now in the House of Lords who proved their eloquence again and again during some of the most important and exciting debates in the representative chamber, and who now hardly open their lips in the gilded chamber, as the House of Lords has been grandiloquently titled. A rising member of the House of Commons succeeds to the family title and estates, and as a matter of course he is transferred to the House of Lords, and there, in most cases, is an end to his public career. Or perhaps a rising member of the House of Commons has in some way or other made himself inconvenient to his leading colleagues who have now come into power and are forming an administration, and as they do not know how to get rid of him gracefully in any other way, they induce the Sovereign to confer on him a peerage, and so he straightway goes into the House of Lords. Perhaps, as he had been an active and conspicuous debater in the House of Commons, he cannot bring himself to settle down into silence when he finds himself among the peers. So he delivers a speech every now and then on what are conventionally regarded in the House of Lords as great occasions, but his career is practically at an end all the same. I have in my mind some striking instances of this curious transition from Parliamentary prominence in the House of Commons to Parliamentary nothingness in the House of Lords. I know of men who were accounted powerful and brilliant debaters in the House of Commons, where debates are sometimes great events, who, when, from one cause or other, translated to the House of Lords, were hardly ever heard of as debaters any more. Probably there seemed no motive for taking the trouble to seek the opportunity of delivering a speech in the hereditary assembly, where nothing particular could come of the speech when delivered, and the new peer allows the charms of public speaking to lose their hold over him, to pass with the days and the dreams of his youth.

Lord Aberdeen would in all probability have made a deep mark as a Parliamentary debater if the kindly fates had left to him the possibility of a career in the House of Commons. He has a fine voice, an attractive presence, and a fluent delivery; he has high intellectual capacity, wide and varied culture, and much acquaintance with foreign States and peoples. Probably the best services which Lord Aberdeen could render to his country would be found in such offices as Ireland and Canada gave him an opportunity of undertaking; viceroyalty of some order, it would seem, must be the main business of his career. But I must say that I should much like to see his great intellectual qualities, his varied experience, and his noble humanitarian sympathies provided with some opportunity of exercising themselves in the work of domestic government. I may explain that I do not call the administration of Ireland under the old conditions a work of domestic government in the true sense. The vice-regal system in Ireland is a barbaric anachronism, and the abilities and high purposes of a man like Lord Aberdeen were wholly thrown away upon such work. There is much still in the social condition of England which could give ample occupation to the administrative abilities and the philanthropic energies of Lord Aberdeen. The work of decentralization in England is rapidly going on. The development of local self-government is becoming one of the most remarkable phenomena of our times. Parliament is becoming more and more the fount and origin of national rule, but it is wisely devoting its energies to the creation of a system which shall leave the working out of that national rule more and more to localities and municipalities. At one time, and that not very long ago, it was believed even by many social reformers that, while self-government might easily be developed in the cities and towns, it would not be possible, during the present generation at least, to infuse any such principle of vitality into the country districts.

Of late years, however, it is becoming more and more apparent that the principle of local government is developing itself rapidly and effectively in the rural districts, and that the good old times when the squire and the rector could manage by divided despotism the whole business of a parish are destined soon to become a curious historical memory. The system of national education, established for the first time in England by Gladstone's Government in 1870, has naturally had much to do with the quickening of intelligent activity all over the British Islands. A new generation has grown up, in which localities are no longer content to have all their business managed for them by their local magnates, and the recent statutes passed by Parliament for the extension everywhere of the local government principle are a direct result of the legislation which has made education compulsory in these countries. All over the agricultural districts we now find county boards and parish councils conducting by debates and divisions the common business of each district, just as it is done in the great cities and towns. It seems to me that this spread of the principle of local self-government opens a most appropriate field for the intellect and the energies of such statesmen as Lord Aberdeen. Only in recent times have great noblemen condescended to trouble themselves much, so far at least as their Parliamentary careers were concerned, with municipal or other local affairs. A peer, if he happened to have any taste or gift for Parliamentary and official work, was willing to become Foreign Secretary, Viceroy of India, Lord-Lieutenant of Ireland, or Governor of a Colony. Not infrequently, too, he consented to devote his energies to the office of Postmaster-General. But he was not likely to see any scope for a Parliamentary career in the management of local business. In his own particular district, no doubt, he was accustomed to direct most of the business in his own way and might be a local benefactor or a local mis-manager, according as his tastes and judgment qualified him. But the general business of localities did not create any Parliamentary department which seemed likely to deserve his attention. The condition of things is very different now, and Lord Aberdeen is one of the men to whom the country is mainly indebted for that quickening and outspreading of the local self-governing principle which is so remarkable and so hopeful a phenomenon of our national existence at present. In every movement which pretends to the development and the strengthening of that principle Lord Aberdeen has always taken a foremost part.

I am not myself an unqualified admirer of that part of the British constitutional system which makes the House of Lords one of three great ruling powers. I should very much doubt whether Lord Aberdeen himself, if he were set to devise a constitutional system for these countries, would make the House of Lords as at present arranged a component part of our legislative system. But I am quite willing to admit that, since we have a House of Lords and while we have a House of Lords, a man like the Earl of Aberdeen does all that can be done to turn the existing constitution to good account and make it in some degree worthy of national toleration. While there exists an aristocracy of birth, even the most uncompromising advocate of democracy and the equal rights of men might freely admit that a career like the political and social career of Lord Aberdeen does much to plead in defense of the system. Lord Aberdeen has always proved that he thoroughly understands the responsibilities as well as the advantages of his high position. Not one of the Labor Members, as they are called, of the House of Commons—the chosen representatives of the working classes—could have shown a deeper and more constant sympathy with every measure and every movement which tends to improve the condition and expand the opportunities of those who have to make a living by actual toil. Lord Aberdeen has yet, I trust, a long and fruitful career before him. The statesmanship of England will soon again have to turn its attention to the social movements which concern the interests of the lowly-born and the hard-working in these islands. If a better time is coming for the statesmen of England, whether in office or in opposition, who love peace and who yearn to take a part in measures which lead to genuine national prosperity, we may safely assume that in such a time Lord Aberdeen will renew his active career, to the benefit of the people whom he has served so faithfully and so well.

*Photograph copyright by W. & D. Downey*
**JOHN BURNS**

# JOHN BURNS

John Burns stands out a distinct and peculiar figure in the House of Commons. He is the foremost representative of that working class which is becoming so great a power in the organization of English political and industrial life. "Be not like dumb driven cattle," says Longfellow in his often-quoted lines—"Be a hero in the strife." The British workingmen were until very lately little better than dumb driven cattle; in our days and under such leadership as that of John Burns they have proved themselves capable of bearing heroic part in the struggle for great reforms. I can remember the time when the House of Commons had not in it any member actually belonging to the working classes. At that time the working classes had no means of obtaining Parliamentary representation, for it may be said with almost literal exactness that no workingman had a vote, or the means of obtaining a vote, at a Parliamentary election. The conditions of the franchise were too limited in the constituencies to enable men who worked for small daily or weekly wages to become voters at elections. In order to become a voter a man must occupy a house rated at a certain yearly amount, and he must have occupied it for a specified and considerable space of time, and there were very few indeed of the working class who could hope to obtain such legal qualifications. In more recent days the great reformers of these islands have succeeded in establishing what may be fairly described as manhood suffrage in these countries, and have also secured a lodger franchise; have established the secret ballot as the process of voting; and by these and other reforms have put the workingman on a level with his fellow-citizens as a voter at Parliamentary elections. My own recollection goes back to the time when the law in Great Britain and Ireland insisted on what was called a "property qualification" as an indispensable condition to a candidate's obtaining a seat in the House of Commons. I have known scores of instances in which clever and popular candidates got over this difficulty by prevailing on some wealthy relative or friend to settle legally on them an amount of landed property necessary to qualify them for a seat in the House. It was perfectly well known to every one that this settlement was purely a formal arrangement, and that the new and nominal possessor of the property was no more its real owner than the child who is allowed for a moment to hold his father's watch in his hand becomes thereby the legal owner of the valuable timepiece. In our days no property qualification of any kind is needed either for a vote at a Parliamentary election or for a seat in the House of Commons, and therefore the workingmen form an important proportion of the voters at Parliamentary elections and are enabled in certain constituencies to choose men of their own class to represent them in the House of Commons.

I have thought it well to make the short explanation of the changes which have taken place in the condition of the British workingmen during recent years as a prelude to what I have to say concerning that foremost of British workingmen, John Burns. It is only fair to say that the workingmen of these countries have made judicious and praiseworthy use of the new political powers confided to them, and have almost invariably sent into Parliament as the representatives of their class men of undoubted ability and of the highest character, men who win the respect of all parties in the House of Commons. Of these men John Burns is the most conspicuous. He has never, indeed, held a place in an administration, as two, I think, of his order have already done; but then John Burns is a man of resolutely independent character, and it would not be easy thus far to form even a Liberal Government which should be quite up to the level of his views on many questions of domestic and foreign policy.

John Burns would hardly be taken personally as a typical representative of the British workingman. He is short in stature, very dark in complexion and in the color of his hair, and a stranger seeing him for the first time might take him for an Italian or a Spaniard. His physical strength is something enormous, and I have seen him perform with the greatest apparent ease some feats of athletic vigor which might have seemed to demand the proportions of a giant. His whole frame is made up of bone and muscle, and although he is broadly and stoutly built, he does not appear to have any superfluous flesh. If I had to make my way through a furious opposing crowd, I do not know of any leader whom I should be more glad to follow than John Burns. But although Burns is physically made for a fighting man, there is nothing pugnacious or aggressive in his temperament. He is by nature kind, conciliatory, and generous, tolerant of other men's opinions, and only anxious to advance his own by fair argument and manly appeals to men's sense of humanity and justice. I have seen him carry a great big elderly man who had fainted at a public meeting and take him to a quiet spot with all the ease and tenderness of a mother carrying her child. But if I were an overbearing giant who was trying his strength upon a weaker mortal, I should take good care not to make the experiment while John Burns was anywhere within reach. He is an adept at all sorts of athletic sports and games, skating, rowing, foot-racing, boxing, cricket, and I know not what else. He is essentially a man of the working class, and has, I believe, some Scottish blood in his veins, but he is a Londoner by birth, and passed all his early life in a London district. He was born to poverty, and received such education as he had to begin with at a humble school in the Battersea region on the south side of London.

Now, I should think that a boy born in humble life who had in him any gift of imagination and any faculty for self-improvement could hardly have begun life in a better place than Battersea. The Battersea region lies south of the Thames, and is a strange combination of modern squalidness and picturesque historical associations and memorials. The homes of the working class poor stand under the very shadow of that famous church in Old Battersea where Bolingbroke, the high-born, one of the most eloquent orators known to English Parliamentary life, and one of the most brilliant writers who adorn English literature, lies buried, and where strangers from all parts of the world go to gaze upon his tombstone. Everywhere throughout the little town or village one comes upon places associated with the memory of Bolingbroke and of other men famous in history. Cross the bridge that spans the Thames and you are in the Chelsea region, which is suffused with historical and literary associations from far-off days to those recent times when Thomas Carlyle had his home in one of its quiet streets. To a boy with any turn for reading and any taste for history and literature, all that quarter of London on both sides of the Thames must have been filled with inspiration. John Burns had always a love of reading, and I can easily fancy that the memories of the place must have been a constant stimulant and inspiration to his honorable ambition for self-culture. His school days finished when he was hardly ten years old, and then he was set to earn a living, first in a candle factory and afterwards in the works of an engineer. Thus he toiled away until he had reached manhood's age, and all the time he was steadily devoting his spare hours or moments to the task of self-education. He read every book that came within his reach, and studied with especial interest the works of men who set themselves to the consideration of great social problems.

Burns naturally became very soon impressed with the conviction that all could not be quite right under a political and social system which made the workingman a mere piece of living mechanism and gave him no share whatever in the constitutional government of the country. At that time there was no system of national education in England, and the child of poor parents had to get his teaching through some charitable institution, or to go without any teaching whatever. So far as the education of the poorest classes was concerned, England was at that time far below Scotland, below Germany and Holland, and below the United States.

As regards the political system, a man of the class to which John Burns was born had little chance indeed of obtaining the right to vote at a Parliamentary election, which was given only to men who had certain qualifications of income and of residence not often to be found among the working classes. The English system of national education is little more than thirty years old, and the extension of the voting power which makes it now practically a manhood suffrage is likewise of very modern date. It was natural that an intelligent and thoughtful boy like John Burns should, under such conditions, become filled with socialistic doctrines and should find himself growing into a mood of impatience and hostility towards the rule of aristocrats, landlords, and capitalists, by which the country was then dominated. Soon after he had reached his twenty-first year he obtained employment as a foreman engineer on the Niger in Africa, and there he had his first experience of a climate and a life totally unlike to anything that could be found in the Battersea regions. I have often heard it said that during his employment in English steamers on the Niger he was known among his British companions as "Coffee-pot Burns," in jocular recognition of his devotion to total abstinence principles. He spent about a year in his African occupation, and during that time he had managed to save up a considerable amount of his pay, a saving which we may be sure was in great measure due to his practice of total abstinence from any drinks stronger than that which was properly contained in the coffee-pot. When he left Africa, he invested his savings in a manner which I cannot but regard as peculiarly characteristic of him, and which must have given to such a man a profitable return for his investment—he spent his savings, in fact, on a tour of several months throughout Europe. Thus he acquired an invaluable addition to his stock of practical observation and a fresh impulse to his studies of life and of books. He settled down in England as a working engineer, and he soon began to take a deep interest and an active share in every movement which had for its object the welfare of the classes who live by daily labor.

Obviously, there are many improvements in the condition of such men which could only be brought about by legislation, and John Burns therefore became a political agitator. His voice was heard from the platforms of great popular meetings held in and around London and in many other parts of the country, and he was one of the leaders of the great agitation which secured for the public the right of holding open-air meetings in Trafalgar Square. John Burns was meant by nature to be a popular orator. He has a physical frame which can stand any amount of exertion, and his voice, at once powerful and musical, can make itself heard to the farthest limit of the largest outdoor meeting in Hyde Park or Trafalgar Square. But he is in no sense whatever a mere declaimer. He argues every question out in a practical and reasonable way, and although he has some views on political and industrial subjects which many of his opponents would condemn as socialistic, there is nothing in him of the revolutionist or the anarchist. His object is to bring about by free and lawful public debate those reforms in the political and industrial systems which he regards as essential to the well-being of the whole community. The Conservative party in this country used to have for a long time one particular phrase which was understood to embody the heaviest accusation that could be brought against a public man. To say that this or that public speaker was endeavoring to "set class against class" was understood to mean his utter condemnation in the minds of all well-behaved citizens. We do not hear so much of this accusation in later days, partly because some of the very measures demanded by those setters of class against class have been adopted by Conservative Governments and carried into law by Conservative votes. But there was a period in the life of John Burns when he must have found himself denounced almost every day in speech or newspaper article as one whose main endeavor was to set class against class. John Burns does not seem to have troubled himself much about the accusation. Perhaps he reasoned within himself that if the endeavor to obtain for workingmen the right of voting at elections and the right to form themselves into trades-unions for the purpose of bettering their lives were the endeavor to set class against class, then there is nothing for it but to go on setting class against class until the beneficent result be obtained. So John Burns went on setting class against class, with the result that he became recognized all over the country as one of the most eloquent, capable, and judicious leaders whom the workingmen could show, and his unselfishness and integrity were never disparaged even by his most extreme political opponents.

A remarkable evidence was soon to be given of the solid reputation which he had won for himself in public life. A complete change was made by Parliamentary legislation in the whole system of London's municipal government. The vast metropolis which we call London was up to that time under the control for municipal affairs of the various parish boards and local vestries, each of them constructed on some representative system peculiarly its own, and none of them, it may be justly said, under any direct control from the great mass of the community. The greater part of the West End of London was under the management of a body known as the Metropolitan Board of Works; the City of London was dominated by its own historic Corporation; each other district of the metropolis had its governing vestry or some such institution. Apart from all other objections to such a system, one of its obvious defects was that no common principle was recognized in the municipal arrangements of the metropolis; there were no common rules for their regulation of traffic, for the levying of rates, for the management of public institutions, and a Londoner who changed his residence from one part of the town to another, or even from one side of a street to another, might find himself suddenly brought under the control of a system of municipal regulations with which he was totally unfamiliar. Appeals were constantly made by enlightened Londoners for some uniform system of London government, but for a long time nothing was done in the way of reform. At last, however, it happened—luckily, in one sense, for the community—that the Metropolitan Board of Works, which ruled the West End districts, became the cause of much public scandal because of its mistakes and mismanagement, not to use any harsher terms, in the dealing with public contracts. The excitement caused by these discoveries made it impossible for the old system to be maintained any longer, and the result was the passing of an Act of Parliament which created an entirely new governing body for the metropolis. This new governing body was styled the London County Council, and it was to have control of the whole metropolis, with the exception of that comparatively small extent of municipal territory which we know as the City of London. The members of the new County Council were to be chosen, for the most part, as are the members of the House of Commons, by direct popular suffrage. Some of the foremost men in England became members of the new County Council. One of these was Lord Rosebery, another was Sir Thomas Farrer (who has since become Lord Farrer), a third was Frederic Harrison, one of the most eminent writers and thinkers of his time, and another was John Burns, the working engineer. I mention this fact only to show how thoroughly John Burns must have established his reputation as a man well qualified to take a leading place in the municipal government of London. Since that time he has been elected again and again to the same position.

When the great dispute broke out in London between the dock-laborers and the ship-owners, John Burns took an active and untiring part in the endeavor to obtain fair terms for the workers, and by his moderation and judgment, as well as by his inexhaustible energy, he did inestimable service in the bringing about of a satisfactory settlement. The late Cardinal Manning took a conspicuous part in the effort to obtain good terms for the workingmen, and he was recognized on both sides of the dispute as a most acceptable mediator, and I remember that he expressed himself more than once in the highest terms as to the services rendered by John Burns during the whole of the crisis. Burns made one or two unsuccessful attempts to obtain a seat in the House of Commons—or perhaps, to put it more correctly, I should say that he consented, in obedience to the pressure of his friends and followers, to become a candidate for a seat. In 1892 he was elected to

Parliament as the representative of that Battersea district where his life began, and he has held the seat ever since. In the House of Commons he has been a decided success. It is only right to say that the workingmen representatives, who now form a distinct and influential section in the House, have fully vindicated their right to hold places there, and have, with hardly any exception, done honor to the choice of their constituents. John Burns is among the foremost, if not the very foremost, of the working class representatives. He has won the good opinions of all parties and classes in the House of Commons. He has won especial merit which counts for much in the House—he never makes a speech unless when he has something to say which has a direct bearing on the debate in progress and which it is important that the House should hear. He is never a mere declaimer, and he never speaks for the sake of making a speech and having it reported in the newspapers. The House always knows that when John Burns rises he has some solid argument to offer, and that he will sit down as soon as he has said his say.

The first time I had the honor of becoming personally acquainted with John Burns was in the House of Commons, shortly after his first election, and I was introduced to him by my friend Michael Davitt. I could not help feeling at the time that it was a remarkable event in one's life to be introduced to John Burns by Michael Davitt. Both these men were then honored members of the House of Commons, and both had for many years been regarded by most of what are called the ruling classes as disturbers of the established order of things and enemies of the British Constitution. Davitt had spent years in prison as a rebel, and Burns had been at least once imprisoned, though but for a short time, as a disturber of public order. Every one came to admit in the end that each man was thoroughly devoted to a cause which he believed rightful, and that the true and lasting prosperity of a State must depend largely on men who are thus willing to make any sacrifice for the maintenance of equal political rights in the community. I have had, since that time, many opportunities of meeting with Burns in public and private and exchanging ideas with him on all manner of subjects, and I can only say that the better I have known him the higher has been my opinion of his intelligence, his sincerity, and his capacity to do the State some service.

John Burns has made himself very useful in the committee work of the House of Commons. The House hands over the manipulation and arrangement of many of its measures on what I may call technical subjects—measures concerning trade and industry, shipping and railways, and other such affairs of business—to be discussed in detail and put into working shape by small committees chosen from among the members; and these measures, when they have passed through this process of examination, are brought up for full and final settlement in the House itself. It will be easily understood that there are many subjects of this order, on which the practical experience and the varied observation of a man like Burns must count for much in the shaping of legislation. Burns has genial, unpretending manners, and although he was born with a fighting spirit, he is not one of those who make it their effort to cram their opinions down the throats of their opponents. Although his views are extreme on most of the questions in which he takes a deep interest, he is always willing to admit that there may be something to be said on the other side of the controversy; he is ever ready to give a full consideration to all the arguments of his fellow-members, and if any one in the committee can show him that he is mistaken on this or that point, he will yield to the force of argument, and has no hesitation about acknowledging a change in his views. Fervent as he is in his devotion to any of the great principles which have become a faith with him, there is nothing of the fanatic about him, and I do not think his enemies would ever have to fear persecution at his hands. There is no roughness in his manners, although he has certainly not been brought up to the ways of what is generally known as good society; and his smile is winning and sweet. He has probably a certain consciousness of mental strength, as he has of physical strength, which relieves him from any inclination towards self-assertion. I should find it as difficult to believe that John Burns countenanced a deed of oppression as I should find it to believe that he sought by obsequiousness the favor of the great.

John Burns was, it is almost needless to say, an opponent from the very beginning of the policy which led to the war against the South African Republics. When the general election came on, about midway in the course of the war, the war passion had come upon the country like an epidemic, and some of the most distinguished English representatives lost their seats in the House of Commons because they refused to sanction the Jingo policy. Many men who were rising rapidly into Parliamentary distinction were defeated at the elections by Imperialist candidates. Nor were the men thus shut out from Parliament for the time all members of the Liberal party. In some instances, although few indeed, there were men belonging to the Conservative, the Ministerial, side, who could not see the justice of the war policy and would not conceal their opinions, and who therefore had to forfeit their seats when some thoroughgoing Tory Imperialists presented themselves as rivals for the favor of the local voters. So great was the influence of the war passion that even among the constituencies where the workingmen were strong there were examples of an Imperialist victory over the true principles of liberty and democracy. But the Battersea constituents of John Burns remained faithful to their political creed and to him, and he was sent back in triumph to the House of Commons to carry on the fight for every good cause there. He took part in many debates during the continuance of the campaign, and he never made a speech on the subject of the war which was not listened to with interest even by those most opposed to his opinions. He has the gift of debate as well as the gift of declamation, and he knows his part in Parliamentary life far too well to substitute declamation for debate. The typical demagogue, as he is pictured by those who do not sympathize with democracy, would on such occasions have merely relieved his mind by repeated denunciations of that war in particular and of wars in general, and would soon have lost any hold on the attention of the House, which is, to do it justice, highly practical in its methods of discussion. John Burns spoke in each debate on the war when he had something to say which could practically and precisely bear on the subject then under immediate consideration—a question connected with the administration of the campaign, with the manner in which the War Office or the Colonial Office was conducting some particular part of its administrative task, with the immediate effects of this or that movement, and in this way he compelled attention and he challenged reply. I remember, for instance, that when the spokesmen of the Government were laying great stress on the severity and injustice of the Boer State's dealings with the native populations of South Africa, John Burns gave from his own experience and observation instances of the manner in which African populations had been dealt with by British authorities, and demanded whether such actions would not have justified the intervention of some European State if the conduct of the Boer Government, supposing it to be accurately described, was a justification for England's invasion of the Boer territory. Whenever he took part in the debate, he met his opponents on their own ground, and he challenged their policy in practical detail, instead of wasting his time in mere declamatory appeals to principles of liberty and justice which would have fallen flat upon the minds of those who held it as their creed that Imperial England was free to dictate her terms to all peoples of inferior strength and less highly developed civilization.

John Burns has fairly won for himself an honorable place in the history of our time. If he had done nothing else, he would have accomplished much by demonstrating in his own person the right of the workingman to have a seat in Parliament. One finds it hard now to understand how the English House of Commons could ever have been regarded as the representative ruling body of England, when it held no members who were authorized by position and by experience to speak for the working populations of the country. I mean no disparagement to the other representatives of the working classes when I say that I regard John Burns as the most distinguished and the most influential among them. Others of the same order have rendered valuable service, not merely to their own class, but to the State in general since they came to hold seats in the House of Commons; some have even held administrative office in a Liberal Government, and have shown themselves well qualified for the duties. Not any of them, so far as I can recollect, has ever shown himself the mere declaimer and demagogue whom so many Conservative observers and critics used to tell us we must expect to meet if the workingmen were enabled to send their spokesmen into the House of Commons. I do not know whether John Burns has any ambition to hold a seat in some future Liberal Ministry, but I venture to think that if such should be his fortune, he will prove himself more useful than ever to the best interests of his country. He has never sought to obtain the favor and the support of his own order by flattering their weaknesses, by encouraging them in their errors, or by allowing them to believe that the right must always be on their side and the wrong on the side of their opponents. I fully believe that he has good and great work yet to do.

*Photograph copyright by W. & D. Downey*
**SIR MICHAEL HICKS-BEACH**

# SIR MICHAEL HICKS-BEACH

Sir Michael Hicks-Beach is now, as everybody knows, out of office. *Il reviendra*, no doubt, and in a happier sense, we may trust, than fate allowed to the once famous personage concerning whom the words I have quoted were said and sung throughout France. *Il reviendra* was the burden of the chant composed to the honor of the late General Boulanger and echoed through all the French music-halls at the time when Boulanger got into trouble with the existing government. But Sir Michael Hicks-Beach is a man of very different order from Boulanger, with whom he has, so far as I know, nothing whatever in common except the fact that they were both born in the same year, 1837.

The admirers of Sir Michael Hicks-Beach may take it for granted that he will some time or other return to a high position in an English administration. Whether that administration is to be Liberal or Conservative we must wait for events to show. One can imagine the formation of a Conservative Government which might rise to the level of Hicks-Beach; or one might imagine the formation of a Liberal Government in which Hicks-Beach could see his way to take office; but I think it would be hard to realize the idea of such a man being left out of office or kept out of office for many years. He was, according to my judgment, the most efficient and capable member of the Conservative Government now in office, the Government from which he felt himself compelled to withdraw, or in which, at all events, he was not pressed to continue. He was not a brilliant figure in that Government. He had not the push and the energy and the impressive debating powers of Mr. Chamberlain, and he had not the culture, the grace, and the literary style of Mr. Arthur Balfour. He made no pretensions whatever to the gift of oratory, although he had some at least of the qualities which are needed for oratorical success. His style of speaking is remarkably clear and impressive. No question, however complex and difficult, seems hard to understand when explained by Hicks-Beach. He compels attention rather than attracts it. There are no alluring qualities in his eloquence, there are no graces of manner or exquisite forms of expression; there is a cold, almost harsh clearness enforcing itself in every speech. The speaker seems to be telling his hearers that, whether they agree with him or not, whether they like him or not, they must listen to what he has to say. There is a certain quality of antagonism in his manner from first to last, and he conveys the idea of one who feels a grim satisfaction in the work of hammering his opinions into the heads of men who would rather be thinking of something else if the choice were left to them. "Black Michael" is the nickname familiarly applied to Sir Michael Hicks-Beach in private conversation by the members of the House of Commons, and the nickname has found its way into the columns of "Punch" and other periodicals. The term "Black Michael" does not, we may assume, refer merely to the complexion of Hicks-Beach, to the color of his hair; but means to suggest a grim dark-someness about his whole expression of countenance and bearing. Certainly any one who watches Sir Michael Hicks-Beach as he sits during a debate in the House of Commons, waiting for his turn to reply to the attacks on some measure of which he is a supporter, will easily understand the significance of the appellation. Hicks-Beach follows every sentence of the speaker then addressing the House with a stern and ironical gaze of intensity which seems already to foredoom the unlucky orator to a merciless castigation. I must say that if I were a member of the House of Commons devoted to the championship of some not quite orthodox financial theory, I should not like to know that my exposition of the doctrine was to be publicly analyzed by Sir Michael Hicks-Beach.

Yet Hicks-Beach is not by any means an ungenial man, according to my observation. Some of his colleagues say that he has a bad temper, or at least a quick temper; and I must say that I can easily understand how a man of vigorous intelligence and expansive views might occasionally be brought into a mood of unphilosophic acrimony by the goings-on of the present Conservative administration. During my many years of service in the House of Commons I had opportunities of coming into personal intercourse with Hicks-Beach, and I have always found him easy of approach and genial in his manners. At different times while he was holding office I had to make representations to him privately with regard to some difficulty arising between an administrative department and certain localities which felt themselves oppressed, or at least put at a disadvantage, by the working of new regulations. I always found Sir Michael Hicks-Beach ready to give a full and fair consideration to every complaint and to exercise his authority for the removal of any genuine grievance. But I can easily understand that observers who have not had personal dealings with Hicks-Beach and have only observed him as he sits silent, dark, and grim during some debate in the House of Commons, may well have formed some very decided impressions as to his habitual moods and tempers. A member of the House once asked me whether I was aware of the fact that a certain line in one of Macaulay's "Lays of Ancient Rome" was supposed to contain a prophetic description of Sir Michael Hicks-Beach. I gave up the puzzle, and then my friend told me that the description was contained in the lines describing the Roman trumpet-call which tell that

"The kite knows well the long stern swell."

I hope my American readers will not have quite forgotten the meaning of the term "swell," now somewhat falling into disuse, but at one time very commonly employed in England to describe a member of what would now be called "smart society."

Sir Michael Hicks-Beach has held many offices. He has been Under-Secretary for the Home Department, and Secretary to the Poor Law Board; he has been twice Chief Secretary for Ireland, or, to speak more strictly, Chief Secretary to the Lord-Lieutenant of Ireland; and he has been twice Chancellor of the Exchequer. I need hardly say that he was not able to accomplish much during the periods of his Irish administration. I have said in preceding articles that it is not possible for the Chief Secretary of a Conservative Government to accomplish anything worth attempting in the work of Irish administration. What Ireland demands is the right to manage her own national affairs in her own domestic Parliament, and there is nothing worth doing to be done by any government which will not take serious account of her one predominant claim. No patronage of local charities, local flower shows, and local racecourses, no amount of Dublin Castle hospitalities, no vice-regal visits to public schools and municipal institutions, can bring about any real improvement in the relations between Great Britain and Ireland. I have no doubt that Hicks-Beach did all in his power to see that the business of his department was efficiently and honestly conducted in Dublin Castle, but under the conditions imposed upon him by Conservative principles it was impossible for him to accomplish any success in the administration of Irish affairs. It has often come into my mind that a certain sense of his limitations in this way was sometimes apparent in the bearing and manner of Sir Michael Hicks-Beach, when he had to take any prominent part in the business of Dublin Castle. He has an active mind and a ready faculty of initiative, and there was no place for such a man in the sort of administrative work which mainly consists in the endeavor to keep things going as they have been going, and striving after an impossible compromise between despotic principles and a free constitutional system.

Hicks-Beach, of course, was more in his place when at the head of the financial department of the administration. He is admitted to have been one of the most skillful and enlightened among modern Chancellors of the Exchequer. His financial statements were always thoroughly clear, symmetrical, and interesting from first to last. He never got into any entanglement with his figures, and his array of facts was always marshaled with something like dramatic skill. I do not profess to be very strong upon financial questions, but I could always understand and follow with the deepest interest any financial exposition made by Hicks-Beach. He seemed to me to be distinctly above the level of his party and his official colleagues on all such questions, and it has often occurred to me that such a man was rather thrown away upon a Conservative Government. Whatever else might be said against them, it could not be said that his speeches at any time sank to the level of the commonplace. There was something combative in his nature, and his style of speaking, with its clear, strong, and sometimes almost harsh tones, appeared as if it were designed in advance to confront and put down all opposition. The House of Commons had for a long time got into the way of regarding Hicks-Beach as a man in advance of his colleagues on all subjects of financial administration. Every Tory in office, or likely to be in office, now professes himself a free-trader, in the English sense of the phrase, but Sir Michael Hicks-Beach was evidently a genuine free-trader, and never could have been anything else since he first turned his attention seriously and steadily to financial questions. I should describe him as one of the foremost debaters in the House of Commons among the men who made no pretensions to the higher order of eloquence; and probably an additional attraction was given to his speeches by that aggressive and combative tone which I have just noticed. I have sometimes fancied that his combativeness of manner and his dictatorial style were less intended for the discomfiture of his recognized political opponents than for that of his own colleagues in office. Long before there was any rumor of incompatibility between Hicks-Beach and the members of the present Government, I have often found myself wondering how the man who expressed such enlightened ideas on so many financial and political questions could possibly get on with a somewhat reactionary Conservative administration. Of course I have no means of knowing anything beyond that which is known to the general public concerning the causes which led to Hicks-Beach's withdrawal or exclusion from his place in the present Government. Even those London journals which profess to know everything about the inner councils of the Cabinet did not, and do not, tell us anything more on this particular subject than the news, impossible to be concealed, that Sir Michael Hicks-Beach had ceased to be a member of the Conservative administration. We were all left to make any conjectures we pleased as to the cause of this remarkable change, and I feel, therefore, no particular diffidence in expounding my own theory. During the long debates on Hicks-Beach's latest Budget proposals, which I had to follow only through the medium of the newspaper reports, I became possessed with the idea that Hicks-Beach was performing reluctantly an uncongenial and almost intolerable task.

Let me recall to the minds of my readers some of the conditions amid which Hicks-Beach found himself compelled of late to carry on his work. It should be said, in the first instance, that he never showed himself, and, as I believe, never could have been, a genuine Tory of the old school. He never exhibited himself as an uncompromising partisan on any of the great subjects which arouse political antagonism. He must have had very little sympathy indeed with the dogmas and the watchwords and the war-cries of old-fashioned militant Toryism. He never identified himself with the cause of the Orangemen in Ireland or the principles of the Jingoes in England. He seldom addressed the House of Commons on any subjects but those which belonged to his own department, and these were for the most part questions of finance. When, however, he had occasionally to take part in debates on subjects connected with England's foreign policy, he generally spoke with an enlightenment, a moderation, and a conciliatory tone which would have done credit to any statesman and seemed little in keeping with the policy and the temper of modern Toryism. But Hicks-Beach had fallen upon evil days for a man of his foresight, his intellect, and his temperament generally who had found a place in a Conservative Cabinet. The policy which led to the outbreak of the war in South Africa aroused a passion in the English public mind which found its utmost fury among the partisans of Toryism. Tory and Jingo became for the time synonymous terms. The man who did not allow his heart and soul to be filled with the war spirit must have seemed to most of his friends unworthy to be called a Conservative. Even among certain sections of the Liberals it required much courage for any man to condemn or even to criticise with severity the policy which had led to the war. Any one who ventured on such a course, whether he were Liberal or Conservative, was straightway branded with the opprobrious epithet of pro-Boer, and that title was supposed to carry his complete condemnation. England had come back suddenly to the same kind of passionate temper which prevailed during the earlier part of the Crimean War. "He who is not with us is against us," cried the professing patriots at both times—he who does not glorify the war is a traitor to his own country and a pro-Boer, or a pro-Russian, as the case might be. This was the temper with which Hicks-Beach found that he had to deal during the later years of his financial administration.

It would be out of place to enter into any speculation as to what Hicks-Beach's own views may have been with regard to the whole policy of the war. It is now well known that Queen Victoria was entirely opposed to that policy, although she did not feel that her position as a constitutional sovereign gave her authority to overrule it by a decision of her own. There is very good reason to believe that peace was brought about at last by the resolute exercise of King Edward's influence. It is at least not unlikely that a man of Hicks-Beach's intellect and temperament may have been opposed at first to the policy which brought on the war, but may have, nevertheless, believed that his most patriotic course would be to remain in the Government and do the best he could for the public benefit. He soon found himself compelled to perform as disagreeable a task as an enlightened financial statesman could have to undertake—the task of extracting from the already overburdened taxpayers the means of carrying on a war of conquest with which he had little sympathy. It was perfectly evident that the needed revenue could not be extracted from the country without some violation of those financial principles to which Hicks-Beach had long been attached. There was no time for much meditation—the money had to be found somehow—and a great part of it could only be found by the imposition of a duty on foreign imports. We now know from public statements made by Sir Michael Hicks-Beach himself that while the war was going on he became impressed with the conviction that the whole administration of the military department was grossly mismanaged, and that the money of the nation was thrown away when the War Office came to spend it. The conviction thus forced upon him could not have tended to make the task of providing means for such further expenditure any the more agreeable to him. We may assume that he saw no other course before him than to make the best of a bad job and try to find in the least objectionable way the amount of money necessary to carry on the business of the State. It was evident to him that the principles of free trade must be put aside for the present, and he found himself driven to the odious necessity of imposing a duty on the importation of foreign corn, a duty which in fact amounted to a tax on bread. Hicks-Beach well knew that no tax could be more odious to the poorer classes of the British Islands; but we may presume that in his emergency he could see no other way of raising the money, and he accepted the situation with a dogged resolve which made no pretense at any concealment of his personal dislike for the task. His manner of delivering the speech in which he set forth his scheme of finance was that of a man who has to discharge an odious duty, or what he finds himself by the force of circumstances compelled to regard as a duty, but will utter no word which might seem to make out that he has any excuse other than that of hateful necessity. The substance of Hicks-Beach's explanations on this part of his budget might be summed up in such words as these: "We have got to pay for this war, and we have no time to spare in finding the money; we must cast aside for the time the principles of free trade; but do not let us further degrade ourselves by hypocritical attempts to make out that what we are doing is in accordance with the free-trade doctrine." I remember well that on reading Hicks-Beach's budget speech I became deeply impressed with the conviction that his task was becoming so intolerable to him that we might expect before long to see a change in the composition of the Government. But it appeared to me that, as the debate went on and the days went on, the position of Hicks-Beach was becoming more and more difficult. Some of the members of the Cabinet became to all appearance suddenly possessed with an inspiration that the time had arrived for a bold movement of reaction against the long-accepted doctrines of free trade. The Chancellor of the Exchequer had already receded so far from the established policy as to propose the imposition of a tax on the imported materials for making bread; and why, therefore, should we not take advantage—thus at least I construed their ideas—of this tempting opportunity to introduce a system of preferential duties and an imitation Zollverein for England and some of her colonies, and to break away from the creed and dogmas of men like Gladstone, Cobden, and Bright? These proposals must have opened to the eyes of Hicks-Beach a vista of financial heresies into which he could not possibly enter. He probably thought that he had gone far enough in the way of compromise when he consented to meet immediate emergencies by the imposition of a bread-tax. Is it possible that he may have felt some compunctious visiting because of his having yielded so far to the necessities of the moment? However that may be, I take it for granted, and took it for granted at the time, that Hicks-Beach found the incompatibility between his own views as to the raising of revenue and the views beginning to be developed by some of his colleagues becoming more and more difficult to reconcile.

Let me venture on an illustration, although it be not by any means photographic in its accuracy, of the difficulty with which the Chancellor of the Exchequer found himself confronted. Let us suppose Hicks-Beach to be the leader of a pledged society of total abstainers. At a moment of sudden crisis he feels called upon to relax so far the rigidity of the society's governing principle as to allow one of its members who is threatened with utter physical prostration a few drops of alcoholic stimulant. He finds his course cordially approved by some of his most influential colleagues, and at first he is proud of their support. But it presently turns out that they regard his reluctant concession as the opening up of a new practice in their regulations, and they press upon him all manner of propositions for the toleration and even the encouragement of what my friend Sir Wilfrid Lawson, the great English champion of total abstinence, would term "moderate drunkenness." Fancy what the feelings of Sir Wilfrid Lawson would be if by some temporary and apparently needful concession he found himself regarded by those around him as an advocate of moderate drunkenness! Such, I cannot help thinking, must have been, in its different way, the condition to which Sir Michael Hicks-Beach felt himself brought down, when he discovered that his introduction of an import duty on foreign grain was believed by his principal colleagues to be but the opening of a reactionary movement against the whole policy of free trade.

The Government of Lord Salisbury seemed to be in the highest good spirits at the prospects before them. Mr. Chamberlain in especial seemed to believe that the time had come for him to develop an entirely new system of his own for the adjustment of import and export duties. For many weeks the English newspapers were filled with discussions on Mr. Chamberlain's great project for the new British Imperial Zollverein, of which England was to be the head. Numbers of Mr. Chamberlain's Conservative admirers were filled with a fresh enthusiasm for the man who thus proposed to reverse altogether the decisions of all modern political economy laid down by Liberal statesmen and Radical writers. Stout old Tory gentlemen representing county constituencies began to be full of hope that the good old times were coming back.

That was the crisis—so far at least as the official career of Sir Michael Hicks-Beach was concerned for the time. What may have happened in the private councils of the Government we of the outer world were not and are not permitted to know. All that we actually do know is that Lord Salisbury resigned his place as Prime Minister, that Arthur Balfour was called to succeed him in office, and that a new administration was formed in which the name of Hicks-Beach did not appear. There were other changes also made in the administration, but with these I shall not for the present concern myself. The important fact for this article is that Sir Michael Hicks-Beach was no longer Chancellor of the Exchequer. All manner of conjectures were made as to the reasons why Lord Salisbury so suddenly withdrew from the position of Prime Minister, and why he could not be prevailed upon to hold the place even nominally until after King Edward's coronation. I do not suppose that the resignation of Lord Salisbury had anything to do with the fact that Sir Michael Hicks-Beach ceased to be Chancellor of the Exchequer. The vacancies were not made simultaneously, nor did there appear any reason to believe that Hicks-Beach was so closely identified with the political fortunes of Lord Salisbury as to be unable to remain in office when his leader had ceased to hold the place of command. So far as an outsider can judge, it must have been that Hicks-Beach could not get on with the new administration, or that the new administration could not get on with him. My own theory, and I only offer it to my readers as the theory of a mere observer from the outside, is that Hicks-Beach could not stand any more of the reaction towards protection principles—thought he had gone quite as far as any sense of duty to his party could exact from him, and made up his mind that if his colleagues were anxious to go any farther in what he believed to be the wrong direction they must do so without any help or countenance from him.

This theory has taken a firmer hold than ever of my mind since I read the report of a speech lately made by Hicks-Beach weeks and weeks after he had ceased to be Chancellor of the Exchequer. That recent speech might have been made by a member of the Liberal Opposition. Certainly in some of its most important and striking passages it enunciated opinions and laid down doctrines which might have come from almost any of Sir Henry Campbell-Bannerman's colleagues on the front Opposition bench. It denounced extravagant war expenditure at a time when Imperialist politicians were calling out for something very like military conscription, and it insisted that the defense of England by the strength of her navy ought to be the main consideration of English statesmanship. That is a doctrine which used to be proclaimed in distant days by such men as Cobden and Bright, which soon became an accepted principle among all genuine Liberals, but has lately been repudiated by all Imperialists, Liberal or Tory, who seem to think that the one great business of English statesmanship is to turn England into a military encampment. The natural and reasonable conclusion to be drawn from such a speech is that during the last session or two of Parliament Hicks-Beach found it impossible to put up any longer with the reign of Jingo principles in the Cabinet, and made up his mind to set himself free from such a domination. The Tory Government has lost its ablest financial administrator, and Sir Michael Hicks-Beach has regained his position of independence.

The future must tell the story of Hicks-Beach's remaining career. That he has yet an important career before him may be taken for granted if only the fates allow him the ordinary length of man's life. Nothing but absolute retirement from Parliamentary work could reduce such a man to a position of complete neutrality, or could prevent him from having an influence which the leaders of both political parties must take into consideration. He is too strong in debate, too well trained in the business of administration, and too quick in observing the real import of growing political changes, and in distinguishing between them and the mere displays of ephemeral emotion, not to make his influence felt at any great crisis in the conditions of political parties. I hold, therefore, to the hope expressed at the opening of this article, that *il reviendra*—that Sir Michael Hicks-Beach will come back before long to an important place in some administration. The House of Commons could not afford just now to lose the services of such a man, and I take it for granted that Hicks-Beach could not remain long in the House of Commons without being called upon to accept an official position. He is beyond question one of the very ablest men on the side of the Government in that House, and his integrity, his moderation, his capacity to understand the significance of new facts, and his disinterestedness have won for him the respect of all parties in Parliament and outside it. We are, to all appearance, on the eve of great changes in the composition of our political parties. With the close of the war has come to an end that season of Jingoism which brought so many weak-minded Liberals into fascinated co-operation with the Tories. The reaction against Toryism must come, and it will probably bring with it a reconstitution of both parties on the principles which each may consider essential to its character at a time when peace at home gives our legislators a chance of studying the domestic welfare of the people in these islands. It will not be enough then for a public man to proclaim himself Imperialist in order to win the votes of a constituency, or to denounce his rival as a pro-Boer in order to secure defeat for that unlucky personage. The constituencies will begin to ask what each candidate proposes to do for the domestic prosperity of our populations at home, and to demand an explicit answer. Under such conditions, whatever be the reconstitution of parties, I am strongly of opinion that Sir Michael Hicks-Beach will before long begin a new administrative career.

*Photograph copyright by Elliott & Fry*

**JOHN E. REDMOND**

# JOHN E. REDMOND

John Edward Redmond is one of the leading men in the House of Commons just now. He is one of the very few really eloquent speakers of whom the House can boast at the present time. His eloquence is, indeed, of a kind but rarely heard in either House of Parliament during recent years. The ordinary style of debate in the House of Commons is becoming more and more of the merely conversational order, and even when the speaker is very much in earnest, even when he is carried away by the fervor of debate, his emotion is apt to express itself rather in an elevation of the voice than in an exaltation of the style. Among members of the House who may be still regarded as having a career before them I do not think there are more than three or four who are capable of making a really eloquent speech—a speech which is worth hearing for its style and its language as well as for its information and its argument. John Redmond is one of these gifted few; Lloyd-George is another. I have heard some critics depreciate John Redmond's eloquence on the ground that it is rather old-fashioned. If it be old-fashioned to express one's meaning in polished and well-balanced sentences, in brilliant phrasing, and with melodious utterance, then I have to admit that John Redmond is not, in his style of eloquence, quite up to the present fashion, and I can only say that it is so much the worse for the present fashion. It is quite certain that Redmond is accepted by the House of Commons in general as one of its most eloquent speakers and one of its ablest party leaders.

Redmond has already been some twenty years in the House of Commons. He was a very young man when first chosen to represent an Irish constituency in the House. I have noticed that our biographical dictionaries of contemporary life do not agree as to the date of Redmond's birth. Some of the books set him down as born in 1851, while others give the year of his birth as 1856. I think I have good reason for knowing that the latter date is the correct one. Perhaps it ought to bring a sense of gratification to a public man when a dispute arises as to the date of his birth. It may give him a complacent reminder of the fact that certain cities disputed as to Homer's birthplace.

John Redmond comes of a good family, and his father was for a long time a member of the House of Commons. I can remember the elder Redmond very well, and he was a man of the most courteous bearing and polished manners, a man of education and capacity, who, whenever he spoke in debate, spoke well and to the point, and was highly esteemed by all parties in the House. John Redmond was educated at Trinity College, Dublin, studied for the law and was called to the bar, but did not practice in the profession. He was elected to the House of Commons in 1881, and became a member of that National party which had been formed not long before under the guidance of Charles Stewart Parnell. From the time when he first took part in a Parliamentary debate it was evident that John Redmond had inherited his father's graceful manner of speaking, and it was soon discovered that he possessed a faculty of genuine eloquence which had not been displayed by the elder Redmond. John Redmond had and still has a voice of remarkable strength, volume, and variety of intonation, and he was soon afforded ample opportunity of testing his capacity for public speech. It was a great part of Parnell's policy that there should be a powerful Home Rule organization extending itself over all parts of Great Britain, founding institutions in all the principal cities and towns, and addressing audiences indoors and out on the subject of Ireland's demand for domestic self-government. John Redmond soon became one of the most effective organizers of this new movement and one of the most powerful pleaders of the cause on public platforms. The first time I ever heard him make a speech in public was at a great open-air meeting held in Hyde Park. He had to address a vast crowd, and I felt naturally anxious to know what his success might be under such trying conditions for a young speaker. He had then but a slender frame, and his somewhat delicately molded features did not suggest the idea of great lung-power. After his first sentence I felt no further doubt as to his physical capacity. He had a magnificent voice, clear, resonant, and thrilling, which made itself heard all over the crowd without the slightest apparent effort on the part of the speaker. I could not help being struck at the time by the seeming contrast between the boyish, delicate figure and the easy strength of the resonant voice.

During his earlier sessions in the House of Commons Redmond did not speak very often, but when he did speak he made it clear that he had at his command a gift of genuine eloquence. He held office as one of the whips of the Irish National party—that is to say, as one of the chosen officials whose duty it is to look after the arrangements of the party, to see that its members are always in their places at the right time, to settle as to the speakers who are to take part in each debate, and to enter into any necessary communications with the whips of the other parties in the House. Redmond was a man admirably suited for such work. He had had an excellent education; he had the polished manners of good society; he belonged to what I may call the country gentleman order, and could ride to hounds with a horsemanship which must have won the respect of the Tory squires from the hunting counties; and he had an excellent capacity and memory for all matters of arrangement and detail. He attended to his duties as one of the party whips with unfailing regularity, and could exercise with equal skill and effect the influence of persuasiveness and that of official command.

In the early days of the Parnell party there was not, to be sure, any great demand on the marshaling power of the whips over the rank and file of the little army. For a considerable time the whole Parnellite party did not consist of more than ten or a dozen members. These members, however, were compelled to do constant duty, and to maintain the great game of Parliamentary obstruction revived by Parnell at all hours of the day and the night. It was quite a common thing for a member of the party to deliver a dozen or fifteen speeches in the course of a single sitting, and John Redmond had all his work to do in endeavoring to keep exhausted colleagues up to their business and to see that they did not leave the precincts of the House until Mr. Speaker should have formally announced that the day's sitting was over. Redmond's services were of inestimable value during such a period of trial. As the days went on, the Irish constituencies became more and more aroused to the necessity of increasing as far as possible the number of thoroughgoing Parnellites in the House by getting rid, at every election, of the Irish members—Irish Whigs as they were called—who did not go in thoroughly, heart and soul, for the policy of Parnell. Under such conditions the influence and the eloquence of John Redmond were of the most substantial service to his party in the work of stirring up the national sentiment among the Irish populations in the cities and towns of England and Scotland. Before many years had passed, John Redmond was one of the whips of an Irish National party in the House of Commons which numbered nearly ninety members. The increase of official duties thus put upon him and his brother whips did not seem to trouble him in the slightest degree. He was always on duty in the House, unless when he had to be on duty at some public meeting outside its precincts; he was ever in good spirits; could always give his chief the fullest and most exact information as to the conditions of each debate, and the best methods of getting full use of the numbers and the debating strength of the Irish party at any given moment.

During the greater part of this time he had not had much opportunity of cultivating his faculty as a debater, for the whip of a party is understood to be occupied rather in putting other men up to speak than in displaying eloquence of his own, and it was for several years not quite understood by the party that John Redmond was qualified to be and was destined to be one of its most commanding spokesmen. I ought to say that among other duties discharged by John Redmond was the trying and responsible task of traveling on more than one occasion over the United States and Canada and Australia to preach the Home Rule gospel to the Irish populations in those countries and to all others who would listen, and thus to obtain the utmost possible support for the great movement at home. For many sessions, however, John Redmond was regarded by his colleagues in the House as a speaker best heard to advantage on some great public platform outside the Parliamentary precincts, and very few of them indeed had yet formed the idea that he was also qualified to become one of the foremost orators in the representative chamber itself.

I may mention here that Mr. Redmond's intimate knowledge of the rules and practices of the House and his thorough acquaintance with its business ways were, in great measure, due to his having held for a time a place in one of the offices belonging to the House of Commons. He was appointed, before he became a member of the House, a clerk in the Vote Office, a department which has to do with the preparation of Parliamentary documents, the distribution of Parliamentary papers, and other such technical work. The clerkships in these offices are in the gift of the Speaker, are an avenue towards the highest promotions in the official staff of the House, and are usually given to young men who, in addition to high education and a promise of capacity, can bring some Parliamentary or family influence to bear on their behalf. John Redmond had some experience in this Vote Office, and it made him a thorough master of Parliamentary business. I had enjoyed his personal acquaintance for some time before he came into the House as a member, and I had been in the House myself some two years before his election. I remember often seeing him and exchanging a word with him as he stood within the House itself, but just below the line which marks the place where the bar of the House is erected when there is occasion, for any public purpose, to admit a stranger thus far and no farther, in order that he may plead some cause before the House or present some petition. Officials employed in any of the offices belonging to the House are allowed the proud privilege of advancing up the floor of the chamber as far as the chair occupied by the Sergeant-at-Arms, the point at which the bar would be drawn across if occasion should require. Thus I had the opportunity of conversing with John Redmond on the floor of the House itself, before he had yet obtained the right of passing beyond the sacred line of the bar.

I am quite certain that Parnell himself did not, until the great crisis came in the Irish National party, fully appreciate the political capacity of John Redmond. Parnell always regarded him as both useful and ornamental—useful in managing the business of the party, and ornamental as a brilliant speaker on a public platform. But he did not appear to know, and had indeed no means of knowing, that Redmond had in himself the qualifications of a party leader and the debating power which could make him an influence in the House of Commons. The speeches which Redmond made, or rather was "put up" by his leader to make, in the House, had often for their object merely to fill up time and keep a debate going until the moment arrived when Parnell thought a division ought to be taken. But when the great crisis came in the affairs of the party, then Redmond was soon able to prove himself made of stronger metal than even his leader had supposed. The crisis was, of course, when the Parnell divorce case came on, and Gladstone and the Liberal leaders generally became filled with the conviction that it would be impossible to carry a measure of Home Rule if Parnell were to retain the leadership of the Irish National party. I need not go over this old and painful story again; it is enough to say that the great majority of Parnell's own followers found themselves compelled to believe that it would be better for Ireland if Parnell were to resign the leadership and retire into private life for a certain time. This Parnell refused to do, and, in opposition to the earnest wishes of the majority of his followers, he published a sort of manifesto in denunciation of Gladstone. Then came the famous meetings of the Irish party in Committee-Room No. 15—one of the committee-rooms belonging to the House of Commons—and, after long days of angry and sometimes even fierce debate, the great majority of the party declared that they could no longer follow the leadership of Parnell. The minority made up their minds to hold with Parnell for good or evil.

I am willing and always was willing to render full justice to the motives which inspired the action of the minority. They did not feel themselves called upon to justify every act of Parnell's private life, but they took the position that his private life had nothing to do with his political career, and that they could not abandon the leader who had done such service to Ireland merely because his name had become associated with a public scandal. On the other hand, the majority of the party, of whom I was one, held that their first duty was to their country, and that if the continued leadership of Parnell rendered it impossible for Gladstone to carry his Home Rule measure, they had to think only of their country and its national cause. During all these debates in Committee-Room No. 15, John Redmond took the leading part on the side of the minority. He became the foremost champion of Parnell's leadership. This position seemed to come to him as if in the nature of things. I well remember the ability and eloquence which he displayed in these debates, and the telling manner in which he put his arguments and his appeals. The course he took was all the more to his credit because Parnell had never singled him out as an object of especial favors and, indeed, in the opinion of many among us, had not done full justice to his services in the House of Commons. Then came the formal division of the party. The majority met together and reconstituted the party with a new Chairman, while the minority associated themselves with Parnell as their leader for the purpose of going over to Ireland and endeavoring to organize the country in his support. When the end of the fierce open controversy was brought about at last by Parnell's sudden death, John Redmond was made the leader of the minority, and from that time forth he began to give more and more distinct evidences of his capacity for a Parliamentary leader's position. He and his group of followers kept themselves in the House of Commons entirely apart from their former colleagues. John Redmond had often to take a part in the debates of the House, and every one could see that the serious responsibility imposed on him was developing in him qualities of leadership, and even of statesmanship, which very few indeed had previously believed to be among his gifts.

Meanwhile the state of things created in Ireland by the split and the setting up of two opposing parties was becoming intolerable. Every man of patriotic feeling on either side of the controversy was coming to see more keenly every day that the maintenance of such a division must be fatal to the cause, for at least another generation. Some efforts were made by the leading men on both sides to bring about a process of reconciliation. John Dillon on the one side, and John Redmond on the other, lent every help they could to these patriotic efforts. John Dillon had by this time become leader of the more numerous party, having been chosen to that position when the leader elected after the severance from Parnell had been compelled by ill health to resign the place. Every reasonable man among the Irish Nationalists, inside and outside Parliament, was coming more and more to see that there was no longer any occasion whatever for further severance, and that the country demanded a return to the old principle of union in the National ranks. John Dillon became impressed with the conviction that it might tend to smooth matters and to open a better chance for reconciliation if he, as one of the most conspicuous anti-Parnellites, were to resign his position, and to invite the whole party to come together again and elect a leader. Dillon was strongly of opinion that, as all matter of controversy had been buried in the early grave of Parnell, it would be better for the cause of future union that the new leader should be chosen from among the small number of men who had always adhered to Parnell's side. Dillon prevailed upon most of his friends to adopt his views on this subject. It was the custom of the Irish National party—indeed, of both the parties—to elect their leader at the opening of each session, and John Dillon had been re-elected more than once to the position of command in his own party. Accordingly, at the close of a session Dillon announced his intention to resign the place of leader, and he added to the announcement that he would not then accept re-election, even if it should be offered to him by a vote of his party. This patriotic course of action was most happy in its results. The Irish National members met together once again as a united party, and the leadership was conferred on John Redmond as an evidence alike of the confidence which was felt in his capacity and his sincerity, and a proof of the desire entertained by the majority for a thorough and cordial reunion of the whole party.

John Redmond was therefore the first leader of the whole party since the events of Committee-Room No. 15. John Dillon and his immediate predecessor had been only leaders of a majority, and now John Redmond was chosen as the leader of the whole party representing the Irish National cause in the House of Commons. He settled down at once to his new position with a temper and spirit admirably suited to the work he had to undertake. He seemed to have put away from his mind all memory of disunion in the party, and he became once more the friend as well as the leader of every member enrolled in its ranks. Many of those who formed the majority had in the first instance only yielded to the persuasion of John Dillon and others in the election of Redmond as leader merely because they believed that by such a course the interests of the cause could best be served just then. But I know that some of these men accepted with personal reluctance what seemed to be the necessity of the hour, and looked forward with anything but gratification to the prospect of having to serve under the new chief. John Redmond, while defending the cause of the still living Parnell, had shown in the service of his chief an energy and a passion which few of us could have expected of him, and was often utterly unsparing in his denunciation of the men who maintained the other side of the controversy. It was not unnatural that many of his former opponents should feel some doubt as to the possibility of working harmoniously under the leadership of a man who had been but lately so bitter an opponent. I had, at the time of the new leadership, been compelled by ill health to give up all active part in public life, but I talked with many members of the majority in the Irish party who told me frankly that they feared it would not be possible to get on under the leadership of John Redmond. Before long, however, these same men spontaneously assured me that they had changed their opinions on that subject, and were glad to find that they could work with Redmond in perfect harmony, and that his manner and bearing showed no sign whatever of any bitter memories belonging to the days of internal dispute. Redmond devoted himself absolutely to the House of Commons and the business of leadership, unless indeed when some pressing national interests compelled him to leave his place in St. Stephen's in order to see to the organization of the National cause in Ireland or in the United States. At the time when I am writing this article he has but lately returned from a visit of that kind to some of the great cities of the American Republic.

Fortunately for his country as well as for himself, John Redmond is a man of private means, is not compelled to earn a living, and can devote the whole of his time to the service of the National cause. He is always to be found at his post while the House of Commons is sitting, and I believe that his morning ride in Hyde Park with his wife every day is one of the few recreations in which he allows himself to indulge. I had not long ago a visit from a well-known member of the Irish Parliamentary party who holds one of its official positions and was at the time of the internal dispute an uncompromising opponent of Parnell's continued rule. This friend of mine I know was decidedly opposed at first to the election of John Redmond as leader, for the reason that he did not believe such an arrangement could possibly work with smoothness and satisfaction to the party. But when I saw him lately, he assured me that he had entirely changed his opinions and that he did not believe any party could possibly have a better leader than John Redmond had already proved himself to be. He had nothing but praise for Redmond's bearing and ways, for the manner in which he appeared to have banished from his mind all memory of past disunion, and for the unremitting attention with which he devoted himself to the work of the party inside and outside the House of Commons.

Since then I have heard and read nothing but good accounts of the manner in which Redmond has reorganized the party. It has under his guidance become once again a powerful force in political life. The House of Commons, as a whole, has thoroughly recognized Redmond's position, influence, and capacity. The Prime Minister has given many proofs of the importance which he attaches to Redmond's decisions and movements. The new leader of the Irish party has won a much higher rank as a Parliamentary debater than he ever had attained to in the days before he had become invested with a really grave responsibility. The newspaper critics on all sides of political life are agreed in describing him as one of the foremost living debaters. Indeed, there are but three or four men in the House of Commons who could possibly be compared with him for eloquence and skill in debate, and there is a quality of grace and artistic form in his style of eloquence which often recalls the memories of brighter days, when the art of oratory was still cultivated in Parliament. The success with which he has conducted the movements of his party has compelled Ministerialists and Opposition alike to take serious account of Redmond and his followers when the chances of any great political measure are under consideration. Only quite lately, during the passage of the Education measure, he adopted a policy which at first greatly puzzled his opponents, and at the last moment succeeded in impressing the Government and the Ministerial party generally with the conviction that Redmond understands when and how to strike a decisive blow.

Of course we hear sometimes, and of late rather often, about differences in the Irish party itself, and about a threatened secession from John Redmond's leadership. The Tory papers in England, and even some of the journals which are professedly Liberal, made eager use of this supposed dissension, and endeavored to persuade themselves and their readers that Redmond has not a full hold over his followers and over the Irish people. I may tell my American readers that they will do well not to attach the slightest importance to these stories about a threatened secession from the lately reunited Irish National party. In the first place, I never heard of any political party which did not inclose in its ranks some men who could not always be reckoned on as amenable to the discipline which is found necessary in every political organization. There is a considerable number of Liberal members who cannot be counted on to follow at all times the guidance of Sir Henry Campbell-Bannerman. There are many Ministerialists, and some of them very clever men, who have lately been proving that at times they would just as soon vote against Arthur Balfour as with him. But in regard to the Irish party and the members who do not always fall in with the wish of its leader, the actual facts are peculiar. The only members of the party who have lately been showing a tendency to mutiny are, with one exception, men of no account whatever in Ireland's political life. I do not wish to name any names, but I can state with deliberation that almost every one of the mutinous members just now is a man who has not the slightest chance of ever again being sent to represent an Irish constituency in the House of Commons. These men have long since forfeited the confidence of their constituents and their fellow-countrymen. They are perfectly aware of this fact; they know quite well that the next general election will see them put out of Parliamentary life; and, in despair of re-election, they probably think that they might as well make the most of the opportunity for rendering themselves conspicuous or for indulging in eccentricities which now can do them no further harm. It may be taken for granted that at the next general election the National constituencies of Ireland will send to the House of Commons no men who are not prepared to work in complete union with the National party, and to recognize the authority of the leader who has the confidence of his people. I do not care to waste many words on this subject, but I think it right to assure my American readers that they need not attach any serious importance to the doings of five or six men, most of whom are either mere "cranks" or are driven to desperation by disappointed personal ambition.

John Redmond has the confidence of his countrymen in England and Scotland, as well as in Ireland, and we have seen that within the last few months he has obtained full assurance that he enjoys the confidence of his countrymen in the United States, in Canada, and in Australasia. I feel all the more ready to bear my testimony to his merits and his success because of the fact that I was, during a crisis which lasted for some years, in direct opposition to the policy which he felt himself conscientiously bound to adopt. The change of events has released him from any obligation to adhere to such a policy, and I do him the justice to believe that he accepted with the sincerest and most disinterested good will the first genuine opportunity offered for a complete reunion of Irish Nationalists. John Redmond is still young enough to have a career before him, and I feel the fullest confidence in his future.

*Photograph copyright by Elliott & Fry*

**SIR WILLIAM HARCOURT**

# SIR WILLIAM HARCOURT

Every friend and admirer of Sir William Harcourt must have been glad when it was made known that the late leader of the Liberal party in the House of Commons had declined to accept the King's offer of a peerage and was determined to remain in that representative chamber where he had made his political name and won his place of command. Sir William Harcourt would have been thrown away in the House of Lords. He could not have done anything to arouse that apathetic chamber to living importance in the affairs of state, and the House of Commons would have lost its most impressive figure. Sir William Harcourt's political fame was made in the House of Commons, and he is even yet its most distinguished member. I say "even yet" because Harcourt is growing old, and has passed that age of threescore years and ten authoritatively set down as the allotted space of man's life. But he shows no appearance of old age, seems full of energy and vital power, and is as well able to command the listening House of Commons by argumentative speech and impressive declamation as he was twenty years ago. Harcourt's bearing is one of superabundant physical resources, and he has a voice of resonant tone which imposes no tax on the listening powers of the stranger in the farthest gallery. He is a very tall man, would be one of the tallest men in any political assembly, and his presence is stately and commanding. After Gladstone's death he became the leader of the Liberal party in the House of Commons, and he resigned that position only because he could not cordially accept the policy and plans of action undertaken by his leader in the House of Lords, Lord Rosebery. I do not propose to enter at any length into the differences of opinion which separated these two men, but it was generally understood that Lord Rosebery did not see his way to carry out Gladstone's policy for the maintenance of Greece and the Christian populations generally against the blood-stained domination of the Ottoman power in the southeast of Europe. The result of these differences was that Lord Rosebery applied himself to form a Liberal party of his own, which should be what is called Imperialist in its policy, and that Harcourt became merely a member of the Liberal Opposition in the House of Commons. To have won the place of Liberal leader in the representative chamber might well have satisfied the ambition of any man, and to withdraw from that place rather than contribute to any further disagreement in the party did not in any sense detract from Harcourt's influence and fame.

Sir William Harcourt won his earliest distinctions in law and literature rather than in politics. He comes of a family which has a history of its own and had members who won reputation during many generations. He was educated at Cambridge University and obtained high honors there. He was called to the bar in

# SIR WILLIAM HARCOURT

1854, and became Queen's Counsel in 1866. In the meantime he had accomplished some important literary work. He was a writer for the "Saturday Review," then at the zenith of its reputation, and under the title of "Historicus" he contributed a series of letters on important public subjects to the "Times" newspaper which attracted universal attention, were afterwards collected and published in a volume, and found readers in every part of the world where men take interest in the public life of England. He was a leading advocate in some legal causes which excited the profound attention of the whole country, and was already regarded as a man of mark, who might be safely assumed to have a successful career before him. It was generally taken for granted at the time that such a man was certain to seek and find a place in the House of Commons, which of course offers an opening for rising legal advocates as well as for rising politicians. I can remember quite distinctly that to all of us who were watching the careers of promising men it appeared quite certain that Harcourt was not likely to content himself with professional distinction, and that when he entered the House of Commons he would devote himself for the most part to the business of political life. He made one unsuccessful attempt to obtain a seat in the House of Commons as representative of a Scottish constituency, and was more fortunate in his second endeavor, when he was elected to Parliament by the city of Oxford as a Liberal in 1868. Then for a while I personally lost sight of him, for towards the close of that year I began a lengthened visit to the United States, and only learned through the newspapers that he was already winning marked distinction as a Parliamentary debater. When I returned to England in 1871, I found that Harcourt was already regarded as certain to hold high office in a Liberal administration. His first step in that direction was to obtain the office of Solicitor-General in Gladstone's Government.

A story was told of Harcourt at the time—this was in 1873—which I believe to be authentic and is worth repeating. Up to this time he was merely Mr. William Vernon Harcourt, but the usage in Parliamentary life is that the leading law officers of the Crown, the Attorney-General and the Solicitor-General, shall receive the honor of knighthood. It was therefore a matter of course that Mr. Harcourt should become Sir William Harcourt, and bear the title by which he is still known everywhere. The story goes, however, that Harcourt was not much delighted with the offer of a distinction which is commonly conferred upon the mayors of English cities and towns and other such personages of municipal position. Harcourt, as I have said, came of a distinguished English family which had contributed Lord Chancellors and other such exalted dignitaries to the business of the State. He probably had also in his mind the fact that rising men in his own profession who happened to be sons of peers were specially exempted by constitutional usage from the necessity of putting up with knighthood when accepting one of the two legal offices under the Crown. The manner in which this very fact proclaimed the comparative insignificance of the title may have still further influenced Harcourt's objections. Anyhow, he did endeavor to impress upon Gladstone his claim to be exempted from the proffered dignity. Gladstone, however, assured him that it was the recognized constitutional practice to confer a knighthood upon a new Solicitor-General, and that there was no reason why Harcourt should seek dispensation from the honor. "Then," demanded Harcourt—so at least the story is told—"why don't you confer knighthoods on all the members of your Cabinet, and see how some of them would receive the proposition?" I cannot vouch for this story as historical truth, but I can vouch for the fact that it was told everywhere at the time, and received, so far as I know, no contradiction.

Harcourt made his way almost at once to the front rank of Parliamentary debaters. His style was somewhat rhetorical and declamatory, but it was distinctly argumentative, and his speeches contained few passages of mere declamation. He was a hard hitter, one of the hardest in the House, but he hit straight from the shoulder and never gave an unfair blow. He was often very happy in his sarcastic touches, and there was a certain robust and self-satisfied good humor even in his severest attacks on his Parliamentary opponents. The general impression of observers at first was that Harcourt would go in merely for the reputation of a powerful debater in the House of Commons, and would not show any ambition for the steady and severe work of Ministerial office. The public had yet to learn that the highest reputation of the man was to be made by his success as the head of a great Ministerial department. Many observers also formed the opinion that Harcourt had no clear political views of his own, and was merely a sort of free lance ready to accept employment under the most convenient leader. He had entered the House of Commons as a Liberal, and even before he accepted office had always ranked himself as a regular supporter of the Liberal party, but he often made speeches in opposition to the views of extreme Liberals or Radicals—speeches such as might well have been made by some eloquent member of the Tory party. Many of the more advanced Liberals had for some time no confidence whatever in Harcourt's Liberalism, and were often engaged in sharp controversy with him. My own impression is that, up to a certain period in his career, Harcourt had not formed, or troubled himself to form, any very settled opinions on the rising political questions of the day. Upon all the old subjects of political debate, on the controversies which divided political parties in a former generation, his views were, no doubt, quite settled, but then there were many new subjects coming up for discussion, bringing with them new occasions for political division, and it is quite probable that on some of these at least the new Solicitor-General had not quite made up his mind. He had been a close student at Cambridge, and had been elected professor of international law by that University; he had practiced law as an advocate, and had begun to make a reputation for himself as a writer. It is quite probable that he had not yet given any special attention to some of the new questions which the growing development of social and political conditions was calling up for Parliamentary consideration.

Harcourt appears to have accepted as a matter of course, when he entered the House of Commons, the recognized principles inherited by the Liberal party. But there was then, as at most other periods of England's constitutional history, a new and advancing Liberal party beginning to make its influence felt, and not satisfied to abide by the mere traditions and established canons of the older Liberalism. Only a very few even of the advanced Liberals were yet prepared to support and encourage the Irish demand for Home Rule, and on such domestic questions, for instance, as the regulation of the liquor traffic, the Liberal party in general had not made up its mind to any policy other than a policy of mere inaction. I mention these two subjects in particular because they have an especial value in throwing light upon the change which took place more lately in Harcourt's political attitude. Probably at the time when he first entered the House of Commons he had not concerned himself much with the Home Rule question, and had allowed himself to take it for granted, as so many even among Liberal politicians and newspapers would have told him, that the Irish Home Rulers were aiming at the break-up of the Empire. In the same way it is quite possible that he may have given little or no attention to the demand for some new regulation of the liquor traffic, and dismissed the whole subject as a crotchet of Sir Wilfrid Lawson. When, however, he began to study the political life of the House of Commons as an active and a rising member, and when he found that his inclinations and his instincts were leading him into politics and away from law, we can easily understand that he set himself to study with candid judgment the new questions which were beginning to divide the Liberal party. I have often heard Sir William Harcourt accused of inconsistency and even of time-serving, because of his sudden conversion to the principle of some political movement which was at last coming to be accepted by the great Liberal leaders. I do not see any reason whatever to believe that Harcourt can fairly be reproached with inconsistency, or justly accused of any ignoble motive for his adoption of the newer and more advanced opinions. The explanation seems to me quite clear. The university student, the practicing advocate, the professor of international law, adopted a new career and devoted himself to an active part in the work of the House of Commons. Then it was that he studied for the first time with earnestness and impartiality some great developing questions which had previously been mere names and shadows to him, and thus he came to form the conclusions which guided his subsequent career. If Harcourt had been thinking chiefly of his own political advancement, he might have done better for himself by following the example of Disraeli, and taking a place among the Tories, where intellect and eloquence were more rare than on the other side of the House, and where promotion was therefore more easily to be won.

Harcourt had probably not given much attention to great financial questions until he came under the influence of Gladstone. Up to that time he had, perhaps, not assumed that such subjects were likely to come within the scope of his practical work; but when he had to study them, he began to discover that he had within him the capacity for a thorough comprehension of their real meaning and development, and as the result of the study he became, when the opportunity offered itself, one of the most successful and enlightened financial Ministers of his time. In the same way he may never have given any serious thought to the question of Irish Home Rule, and may have fallen quietly into the way of regarding it, in accordance with the common opinion of most Englishmen just then, as something naturally associated with a rebellious desire for the breaking up of the Empire. When, however, he was led to study it as a question of reasonable import, he grew to be a convinced and a hopeful advocate of the cause. For a long time after he had taken office under Gladstone he found himself brought into an incessant opposition and even antagonism to the small group of Irish members, who then represented the Irish national demand, and compelled to fight against the obstruction which these

Irish members were raising night after night, as their only means of enforcing public attention to a serious consideration of Ireland's national complaints and claims. He became converted to the cause of Home Rule, just as Gladstone did, by having the question forced upon his consideration, and thus being compelled to ask himself whether there was not some real sense of justice inspiring the Irish agitation.

I shall always remember a conversation I once had with Gladstone on this subject of Irish Home Rule. It was in one of the inner lobbies of the House of Commons, and Mr. Gladstone began it by asking me how I could regard Home Rule as a national demand, seeing that only a very small number of the Irish representatives in the House were actively in favor of such a measure. Gladstone called my attention to the fact that out of the whole body of Irish representatives elected by the constituencies on the same basis of voting, less than a dozen members declared themselves uncompromising advocates of Home Rule. I drew Gladstone's attention to the fact that the suffrage in Ireland was so high and so restricted that the whole bulk of the Irish population were disqualified by law from giving a vote at any election. Gladstone appealed to me to say whether he had not long been in favor of an expanded suffrage for the whole Kingdom, and I told him that I cordially recognized his sincere purpose, and that whenever we got a really fair and popular suffrage he would then find ample proof that the great bulk of the Irish people were united in their demands for Home Rule. Not long after, it came about that Gladstone and his Government saw their way to a measure of reform which gave the whole Kingdom an expanded and popular suffrage, and at the next general election the great majority of Irish members opposed to or lukewarm about Home Rule disappeared altogether from Parliament, and their places were taken by avowed and uncompromising Home Rulers elected mainly because they were earnest advocates of Home Rule. Out of the hundred and three members who constitute the Irish representation, we had then nearly ninety who were proclaimed and consistent Home Rulers. This result did much of itself to make Gladstone a convert to Home Rule, and it had naturally the same effect on Harcourt, who was far too intelligent a man not to accept the lesson taught by the Irish constituencies, and to admit that the demand for Home Rule was a genuine national demand, and as such entitled to the serious consideration of real statesmen. The conversion of Harcourt I have always, therefore, regarded as sincere and statesmanlike, and of the same order as the conversion of Gladstone himself. The first business of statesmanship is to recognize established facts and to act upon their evidence. Once the demand had been proved to be national, neither Gladstone nor Harcourt was the man to deny it a full consideration; and the same full consideration made the one man and the other an advocate of Home Rule.

In the days before the great constitutional change which I have described, the change which resulted in the adoption of a popular suffrage, in the days when our small band of Irish Nationalists was still doing battle inch by inch against the Government, we had many fierce struggles with Harcourt, then a leading member of the Liberal administration. We had to admit that we found in him a powerful antagonist. He was ready in reply, resolute in maintaining his position, and he gave us, to say the least of it, as good as we brought. He was ever alert, he could answer attack by attack, he could carry the battle into the enemy's ranks, and the ablest of our debaters had his best work to do when compelled to stand up in Parliamentary contest against Harcourt. But I observed that in our private dealings with Harcourt, on questions which came within the range of his administrative functions, we always found him considerate, kind, and even generous. There were frequent occasions when a Minister of the Crown had to be applied to by an Irish member for justice in the dealings of his official department, where individual questions of right and wrong having nothing to do with the general subject of Home Rule came up for consideration. I am now speaking of questions which were not to be settled by mere debate in the House of Commons, but which belonged to the ordinary and practical dealings of the department with this or that individual case. I can remember many instances in which I had to make some such appeal to Sir William Harcourt, and I ever found him most ready and willing to consider fairly the nature of any individual grievance, and to prevent the administration of the law from being perversely turned into an engine of oppression. I know that many of my colleagues as well as myself felt thankful to Harcourt for his prompt interference where a real grievance had been brought under his notice, and for his resolve to see that justice must be done to the obscure sufferer from official tyranny. When the Liberal Government and the Irish National party came to work together for Home Rule, we, the Irish National members, had nothing on our memory which could prevent us from regarding Harcourt as a genuine Liberal and a sincere friend who had never shown any inclination to abuse his power when he was strong and we were at our weakest. My recollection of the days when we were fighting against Harcourt is tinged with no bitterness. He was always a formidable fighter, but he fought fairly when he still had to fight against us.

It is not surprising that Harcourt should have been for some time regarded as a powerful debater and nothing more. He was one of the foremost debaters in the House of Commons, even at a time when that House had more commanding debaters in it than it can claim to have just at present. He cannot be ranked among the great orators of the House. He is wanting in imagination, and without the gift of imagination there cannot be eloquence of the highest order. Even in the mere making of phrases he has seldom shown originality, and it has often been remarked of him, as it was remarked by Disraeli of Sir Robert Peel, that he never ventures on any quotation which has not already well established its popularity. Sir William Harcourt's best qualities as a speaker consist in his clearness of exposition, his unfailing fluency, his masterly array of forcible argument, and the fact that he never allows his eloquence to soar over the heads of his audience. I should be inclined to say of him that, although he is unquestionably a great Parliamentary debater, yet his intellectual capacity, his faculty for balancing evidence, acquiring and comparing facts, appreciating tendencies, and coming to just conclusions, are greater even than his powers of speech. I may say that one who listened to Sir William Harcourt during the earlier stages of his Parliamentary career might very naturally have been led to quite a different conclusion, and might have set him down as a clever maker of speeches and not a statesman. But such an observer, supposing him to be endowed with a fair amount of intelligence, would have gradually changed his opinion as he followed Harcourt's political career. Every time that Harcourt has been in office he has more and more given proof that there is in him the true quality of statesmanship. He served as Home Secretary under Gladstone, and was afterwards Chancellor of the Exchequer, first in one of Gladstone's Administrations and afterwards in the Government of Lord Rosebery. There can be no question that he proved himself to be one of the greatest financial Ministers England has had in recent times. His famous Death Duties budget, introduced while Lord Rosebery was Prime Minister, created one of the most vehement controversies known to the political life of the present generation. Yet the great principle which Harcourt embodied in his dealing with the question of death duties must now be regarded even by his political opponents as resting on a basis of absolute morality and justice. The principle merely was that the amount of taxation which any individual pays to the State in consideration of his having obtained property by bequest shall be greater in proportion according as the acquired property is great in amount. In other words, Harcourt's policy maintained that a man who comes in for a large property as a bequest shall pay a larger proportion of taxation to the State than a man who comes in for a small property, and that the same principle ought to prevail through our other systems of direct taxation. The whole controversy simply turns on the question whether the rich man ought or ought not to pay a larger proportion of his income to defray the national expenses than the poor man—whether the citizen who has only income enough to enable him to maintain his family decently ought to be called upon to pay towards the maintenance of the State on just the same scale as that ordained for the man who can live in lavish luxury. The boldness and originality of Sir William Harcourt's venture in his budget of 1893, the energy and argumentative power with which he carried it to success, have undoubtedly secured for him a place in the front rank of England's financial Ministers. The later years of Harcourt's career offer a strange commentary on the estimate generally formed of him when he began to be conspicuous in Parliament. At the former period he was commonly regarded as a clever but somewhat superficial man, as one whose qualities were rather flashy than sound, as a ready maker of telling speeches designed to produce an immediate effect and destined to be utterly forgotten the day after to-morrow. Harcourt's later years of public work have proved him to be a serious Parliamentary leader, a man of strong and deep convictions, a man who thinks before he speaks and speaks because he thinks.

Indeed, the seriousness of Harcourt's convictions on some subjects of national importance has brought him more than once into disfavor with his constituents. He holds very strong and advanced views on the subject of local option—that is to say, on the right of localities to say whether they will or will not allow the sale of intoxicating drinks within their confines, and to state what conditions are to be imposed on the traffic if it is permitted at all. Sir William Harcourt went further on this subject than some even among his colleagues who were in favor of the general principle as a principle, but did not see the necessity for pressing it to immediate action. One of those colleagues said to me that in his opinion Harcourt might very well have allowed the question to stand over for eight or ten years, and perhaps by the end of that time the habits of the population would have improved so far as to render the passing of any strong restrictive law unnecessary. I am quite certain that Harcourt's earnest resolve to deal boldly with this subject if he should be allowed the opportunity had much to do with the condition of feeling in the Liberal party which led to his resignation of its leadership. We may look forward with confidence to the formation of a new Liberal Government in which Harcourt will have a commanding position, and when that time comes we may take it for granted that, in spite of whatever opposition on either side of the House of Commons, he will once more attempt to deal with the question of local option.

Most of my American readers know that Sir William Harcourt's second wife was the daughter of Lothrop Motley, the famous historian who was for a time Minister to Great Britain, and who died at Harcourt's country residence in 1877. The eldest son, Louis Vernon Harcourt, who was born in 1863, has also married an American lady. Louis Harcourt, whom I have known since his boyish days, is endowed with much of his father's talents, and I have always thought that if he had devoted himself entirely to political life he might make for himself such a career as his father has already accomplished. During contested elections I have been more than once associated with Louis Harcourt in "stumping" some parts of the country on behalf of the Liberal Government then engaged in the cause of Home Rule, and I have the clearest memories of his remarkable organizing capacity, his ready eloquence, and his skill in replying to questions and arguments and in convincing skeptical voters. I take it for granted that every one who has known Louis, or, as he is commonly called, "Lulu" Harcourt, must have delightful recollections of his bright companionship. We have all heard that Sir William Harcourt studiously consulted his son when the offer of a peerage was made to him by King Edward, and that "Lulu" was resolute in supporting his father's desire to refuse the honor, even although his acceptance of it would have made "Lulu" the heir to a peerage. Sir William Harcourt, we may well hope, has yet good work to do in the House of Commons. There is nothing about him which suggests the idea of advanced years or of decaying powers, whether mental or physical. The curious attack of weakness which lately came over so many members of the Liberal party never touched his robust intellect and resolute character. No man could render more valuable services than he may be expected to do in turning to account for genuine Liberalism the reaction already beginning to set in against the reign of the Tories and the Jingoes. I cherish the belief that the best of Sir William Harcourt's work is yet to be done by him.

*Photograph copyright by London Stereoscopic Co.*
**JAMES BRYCE**

# JAMES BRYCE

James Bryce is universally recognized as one of the intellectual forces in the British House of Commons. When he rises to make a speech, every one listens with the deepest interest, feeling sure that some ideas and some instruction are sure to come which no political party in the House can well afford to lose. Some men in the House of Commons have been orators and nothing else; some have been orators and instructors as well; some have been Parliamentary debaters more or less capable; and a good many have been bores. In every generation there have been a few who are especially regarded as illuminating forces. The House does not think of measuring their influence by any estimate of their greater or less capacity for mere eloquence of expression. It values them because of the lessons which they teach. To this small order of members James Bryce undoubtedly belongs. Now, I do not mean to convey the idea that such men as these are not usually endowed with the gift of eloquence, or that they cannot deliver speeches which would entitle them to a high rank among Parliamentary debaters, no matter what the import of the speeches might be. My object is to describe a certain class of men whose Parliamentary speeches are valued by members in general without any special regard for their form, but only with regard to their substance, for the thoughts they utter and not for the manner of the utterance. James Bryce would be considered an effective and even a commanding speaker in any public assembly, but nevertheless, when the House of Commons and the public think of his speeches, these are thought of mainly for the truths they tell and the lessons they convey, and not for any quality of mere eloquence which adorns them. In a certain sense James Bryce might be described as belonging to that Parliamentary order in the front of which John Morley stands just now; but of course John Morley has thus far had more administrative experience than James Bryce, and has taken a more distinct place as a Parliamentary and popular leader. Of both men, however, I should be inclined to say that their public speeches lose something of the praise fairly due to them as mere displays of eloquence, because of the importance we all attach to their intellectual and educational influence.

I may say also that James Bryce is not first and above all other things a public man and a politician. He does not seem to have thought of a Parliamentary career until after he had won for himself a high and commanding position as a writer of history. Bryce is by birth an Irishman and belongs to that northern province of Ireland which is peopled to a large extent by Scottish immigrants. We are all rather too apt to think of this Ulster province as essentially un-Irish, or even anti-Irish in tone and feeling, although some of the most extreme among Irish Nationalists, men like John Mitchell for instance, were born and brought up in Ulster, and in more recent days some conspicuous Home Rulers have sat in the House of Commons as representatives of Ulster constituencies. James Bryce has always been an Irish Nationalist since he came into public life, and has shown himself, whether in or out of political office, a steady and consistent supporter of the demand for Irish Home Rule. Indeed, I should be well inclined to believe that a desire to render some personal service in promoting the just claims of Ireland for a better system of government must have had much influence over Bryce's decision to accept a seat in the House of Commons.

Bryce began his education in the University of Glasgow, from which he passed on to Oxford, where he won many honors and has left the memory of a most successful career, not merely as student, but also as professor. He studied for a while at Heidelberg, where he cultivated to the full his previously acquired knowledge of German; and I have heard in later years on good authority that while Bryce was a member of Mr. Gladstone's Government he became a great favorite with Queen Victoria because of his capacity for fluent speech in the language which the late Queen loved especially to hear. Before he turned his attention to active political life Bryce studied for the bar, became a member of the profession, and actually practiced in the Law Courts for some years. Thus far, however, he had hardly given indication of the gifts which were destined to secure for him a high and enduring place in English literature. Thus far his life may be regarded as that of a student and a scholar; he had yet to give to the world the fruits of his scholarship. James Bryce is probably above all things a scholar. He is, I may venture to say, the most scholarly man in the House of Commons. I doubt whether there is in England so widely read a man in all departments of literature, art, and science as Bryce, now that Lord Acton has been removed from us by death. Long before his entrance into Parliamentary life Bryce had obtained the highest distinction as a writer of history. It is not too much to say that his great historical work, "The Holy Roman Empire," is destined to be an English classic and a book for all countries and all times. The author could hardly add to the reputation he won by this masterpiece of historical study, insight, and labor, but it is only mere justice to say that every work of importance which he afterwards gave to the world has maintained his position in literature. His turn of mind has been always that which distinguishes the practical student—the student of realities, not the visionary or the dreamer, the man who, according to Goethe's phrase, is occupied more by the physical than by the metaphysical. In 1877 he published a narrative of his travels in Transcaucasia, with an account of his ascent of Mount Ararat. I believe no other traveler has ever accomplished such a practical study of Mount Ararat as that which was made by Mr. Bryce, and during a part of his explorings he was absolutely alone, as he could not prevail upon the guides belonging to that region to overcome their superstitious dread of an intrusion on certain parts of the mountain. He was always fond of travel, and was able to bring some fresh ideas out of places long familiar to tourists, and he gave to the world in English periodicals the results of his experiences as a traveler. His descriptions of Icelandic scenery and of some rarely visited regions of Hungary and of Poland have a genuine literary as well as a genuine geographical value.

His most important work, after his great history of the Holy Roman Empire, is undoubtedly his book on "The American Commonwealth," published in 1888. This work has been read as generally and studied as closely on the one side of the Atlantic as on the other. I have heard it spoken of with as thorough appreciation in New York, Boston, and Washington as in London, Manchester, and Liverpool. Many years have passed since an eminent English public man, not now living, expressed to me an earnest wish that some European writer would take up the story of the great American Commonwealth just where De Tocqueville left it in his "De la Démocratie en Amérique." I joined cordially in his ideas and his wishes, and we discussed the qualifications of certain Englishmen for the task if any of them could see his way to undertake it, but neither of us seemed to be quite satisfied that we had named the right man for the work. At the time it did not occur to either of us that the historian of "The Holy Roman Empire" would be likely to turn his attention to the story of the American Commonwealth. Indeed, the two studies seemed to me so entirely different and uncongenial that if the name of James Bryce had been suggested to me at the time I should probably have put it aside without much hesitation. One could hardly have looked for so much versatility even in Mr. Bryce as to favor the expectation that he could accomplish, with something like equal success, two historical works dealing with such totally different subjects and requiring such different methods of analysis and contemplation.

More lately still Mr. Bryce brought out his "Impressions of South Africa." This book was published in 1897, and the time of its publication was most appropriate. It appeared when the prospects of a war with the Transvaal Republic were opening gloomily for the lovers of peace and fair dealing in England. If Mr. Bryce's impressions of South Africa could only have been appreciated, and allowed to have their just influence with the leaders of the Conservative party at that critical time, England might have been saved from a long and futile war, and from much serious discredit in the general opinion of the civilized world. But if Bryce had spoken with the tongue of an angel, he could not at such a time have prevailed against the rising passion of Jingoism and the overmastering influence of mining speculators. It is only right to say that the book was in no sense a mere distended political pamphlet. It was not meant as a counterblast to Jingoism, or as a glorification of the Boer Republic. It was a fair and temperate statement of the author's observations in South Africa, and of the general conclusions to which his experience and his study had brought him. Bryce pointed out with perfect frankness the defects and dangers he saw in the Boer system of government, and even the most ferocious Jingo could hardly have felt justified in describing the author by that most terrible epithet, a "pro-Boer." The warning which Bryce gave, and gave in vain, to the English Government and the English majority, was a warning against the credulous acceptation of one-sided testimony, against the fond belief that the proclamation of Imperialism carried with it the right to intervene in the affairs of every foreign State, and against the theory that troops and gold mines warrant any enterprise.

The Parliamentary career of James Bryce began in 1880, when he was elected as Liberal representative for a London constituency. He did great work in the cause of national education, and took an important part in two State Commissions appointed to conduct inquiries into the working of the public schools. At a later period he was chosen to represent a Scottish constituency, and when Mr. Gladstone came into power as the head of a Government Bryce received the important office of Under-Secretary for Foreign Affairs. At that time his chief, the Secretary for Foreign Affairs, was a member of the House of Lords, and therefore the whole work of representing the department in the House of Commons, where alone any important debates on foreign questions are conducted, fell on Mr. Bryce, who had the entire conduct of such discussions on behalf of the administration. The department was one which gave an effective opportunity for the display of Bryce's intimate knowledge of foreign countries, and he acquitted himself with all the success which might have been expected from one of his intellect, his experience, and his enlightened views. Later still he became Chancellor of the Duchy of Lancaster, and for the first time had a seat in the Cabinet. The Chancellorship of the Duchy of Lancaster is one of a small order of English administrative offices which have comparatively unimportant duties attached to their special administration, and leave the man in possession ample time to lend his assistance, both in the Cabinet and in the House of Commons, to all the great public questions which occupy the attention of the Government. In 1894 he became President of the Board of Trade, one of the most important positions in any administration. Bryce's official career came to a close for the present when the Liberal party lost their majority in the representative chamber, and the Conservatives got into power and secured the administrative position they are holding at the present day. Nothing can be more certain than that the first really Liberal administration which is again formed will assign to Mr. Bryce one of the highest places in its Cabinet and in its work. Since he has come to sit on the benches of Opposition he has taken part in many great debates, and is always listened to with the most profound attention. He is one of the few leaders of the Liberal party who were manful and outspoken in their opposition to the policy which originated and carried on the late South African war. He has taken a conspicuous part in every debate upon subjects of foreign policy, of national education, and of political advancement. He has never acted as a mere partisan, and his intervention in debate is all the more influential as it is well understood that he advocates a policy because he believes it to be right and not because of any effect it may have in bringing himself and his Liberal colleagues back again into power.

    I have often noticed the effect produced in the libraries and committee-rooms, in the rooms assigned to those who dine and to those who smoke, when the news is passed round that Mr. Bryce is on his feet. A member who is reading up some subject in the library, or writing his letters in one of the lobbies, or enjoying himself in a dining-hall or a smoking-room, is not likely to hurry away from his occupation or his enjoyment in order to rush into the debating chamber merely because he is told that some leading member of the Government or the Opposition has just begun to address the House. The man who is addressing an audience in the debating chamber may hold an important office in the Government or may have an important place on the Front Bench of Opposition, but then he may be a personage who feels bound to take part in a debate merely because of the position he holds, and every one knows in advance what views he is certain to advocate and what line of argument he is likely to adopt, and our reading or dining or smoking friend may not think that there is any pressing necessity for his presence as a listener in the House. But there are some leading men on both sides of Mr. Speaker who are always sure to have something to say which everybody wants to hear, and Mr. Bryce is unquestionably one of that happily endowed order. When the word goes round that Bryce is up, everybody knows that something will be said on which he cannot exactly calculate beforehand, something to which it is important that he should listen, and there is forthwith a rush of members into the debating chamber. There can hardly be a higher tribute to a man's importance as a debater than the fact that his rising to address the House creates such an effect, and I have seen it created again and again whenever the news went round that "Bryce is on his legs." I have many a time heard Conservative members murmur, in tones not altogether expressing absolute satisfaction at the disturbing information, "Bryce is up—I must go in and hear what he has to say." The tribute is all the higher in this case because Bryce is not one of the showy and fascinating debaters whom everybody wants to listen to for the mere eloquence and fascination of their oratorical displays. Everybody knows that when he speaks it is because he has something to say which ought to be spoken and therefore ought to be heard. It is known that Bryce will not make a speech merely because he thinks the time has come when some leader of Opposition ought to take part in the debate, if only to show that the Opposition is attending to its business.

This command over the House Bryce has always held since he became one of its members, and no man can hold a more desirable and a more honorable position. It is all the more to his credit because he does not aim at mere originality and never makes it a part of his ambition to say something astonishing and thus to excite and delight the mere curiosity of his audience. There have been and still are many members of the House who have made a reputation of this kind and are therefore always sure to command a full attendance merely because everybody expects that when they rise to their feet they are sure to make the House "sit up," if I may use this somewhat colloquial, not to say vulgar, phrase. Take such a man, for instance, as the late John Arthur Roebuck, a man of great intellect, master of a peculiar style of eloquence, who made himself only too often a splendid specimen of what might be called in American phraseology "a crank." All that could be said with certainty beforehand of Roebuck was that whenever he rose to speak he would say something calculated to startle or to puzzle the House. There are men of the same order, if not perhaps of quite the same debating qualifications, in the House at present—men who always draw a rush of members when they rise to speak because nobody can tell in advance what side they are likely to advocate or what sort of bewildering paradox they may set up and make interesting if not convincing by the force of their peculiar style of eloquence. Bryce is emphatically not a man of this order. He is no lover of paradox; he has no desire to create a sensation; he merely wants to impress the House with what he believes to be the truth, and his great quality is that of a beacon and not of a flashlight. His arguments appeal to the intellect and the reasoning power; he speaks of what he knows; he has large resources of thought, experience, and observation to draw upon, and the listeners feel convinced beforehand that he will tell them something they did not know already, or will put his case in some new and striking light.

The House of Commons well knows that it would lose one of its most valuable instructors if Bryce were no longer to occupy a place on its benches or were to condemn himself to habitual inactivity and silence. When the Conservative Government under Lord Salisbury came into power, and more especially after the late general election which brought them back with added strength, many of the Liberal leaders seemed to have grown weary of the political struggle. Something worse than mere apathy appeared to have set in, something more than mere despondency and disheartenment. Men on whom the Liberals of England had long been wont to rely suddenly showed an apparent loss of faith in all the proclaimed principles of the party, and either relapsed into utter silence or spoke in language which suggested an inclination to cross over to the enemy's camp. The two principal impulses to this mood of mind were the South African war and the Irish Home Rule question. The majority in the constituencies had become inflamed with the spirit of Jingoism, and could think of nothing but the war and the Imperial glory of annexing new territory. Feeble-hearted and weak-kneed Liberals began to think that the party could never hope for a return to power unless it too could blow the Imperial trumpet. Other Liberals made it manifest that they were becoming alarmed by the unpopularity of the Home Rule question, and were repenting the enthusiasm which had carried them too far along the path marked out by the genius and the patriotic resolve of Gladstone. A species of dry-rot appeared to have broken out in Liberalism. Before long a new section of Liberalism was formed, the principle of which appeared to be that its members should call themselves Imperial Liberals, and at the same time should support the Tories on the only important questions then under discussion—the policy of the South African campaign and the Irish National claim for Home Rule. Some of the men who had held high office when Gladstone was in power, who had made themselves conspicuous by the ardor and the eloquence with which they supported his policy of peace abroad and justice to Ireland, now openly avowed their renunciation of his great principles. There were others among the foremost Liberals in the House of Commons who, if they did not thus openly take the renegade part, kept themselves quietly out of the active political field and allowed the movement of reaction to go on without a word of protest. Three at least among the Liberal leaders took a very different course. Three of them, at least, not merely nailed their colors to the mast, but stood resolutely in fighting attitude beneath the colors and proved themselves determined to maintain the struggle. These three men were Sir Henry Campbell-Bannerman, John Morley, and James Bryce. There were others, too, it must be said, who stood up manfully with these three in defense of that losing cause of Liberalism which they could never be brought to regard as a lost cause. But the dauntless three whom I have just mentioned were the most prominent and the most influential who went forth against that great array of Toryism and Jingoism. Bryce was in his place as regularly as ever during the whole of that depressing time, and he never failed to raise his voice when the occasion demanded his intervention on behalf of the true principles and practices of Liberalism. During that long, dreary, and disheartening season when despondent men were often disposed to ask whether there was any longer a Liberal party, Bryce made some of the ablest speeches he has ever delivered in arraignment of the Jingo policy, of the War Office maladministration, and the rule of renewed coercion in Ireland. The Liberal cause in England owes a debt that never can be forgotten to the three men whom I have named, for their unflinching resolve and activity in the House of Commons; and of the three none did better service than that which was rendered by James Bryce.

Bryce has, in face and form, the characteristics of a stalwart fighter. His forehead is high and broad, with strongly marked eyebrows, straightly drawn over deep and penetrating eyes. The features are all finely modeled, the nose is straight and statuesque, the hair is becoming somewhat thinner and more gray than it was when I first knew Mr. Bryce, but the mustache and beard, although they too show some fading in color, are still thick and strong as in that past day. The face does not look Irish; its expression is perhaps somewhat too sedate and resolute; but on the other hand, it does not seem quite Scotch, for there is at moments a suggestion of dreaminess about it which we do not usually associate with the shrewd North Briton. Bryce is a man of the most genial temperament, thoroughly companionable, and capable of enjoying every influence that helps to brighten existence. Always a student of books and of men, he is never a recluse, and I do not know of any one who seems to get more out of life than does this philosophic historian. Bryce's London home is noted for its hospitality, and his dinner parties and evening parties give much delight to his large circle of friends. Mr. and Mrs. Bryce are not lion-hunters, and do not rate their friends according to the degree of celebrity each may have obtained. But they have no need to engage in a hunt after lions, for the celebrities seek them out as a matter of course, and I know of no London house where one is more certain to meet distinguished men and women from all parts of the civilized world. Bryce's travels have made him acquainted with interesting and eminent persons everywhere, and an admission to his circle is naturally sought by strangers who visit London. Representatives of literature, science, and art, of scholarly research, of political movement, and of traveled experience are sure to be met with in the home of the Bryces. I had the good fortune to meet there, for the first time, many distinguished men and women whose acquaintance it was a high and memorable privilege to make. Among Bryce's especial recreations is mountain-climbing, and he was at one time President of the Alpine Club. He can converse upon all subjects, can give to every topic some illustration from his own ideas and his own experiences, and the intelligent listener always finds that he carries away something new and worthy of remembrance from any talk with him. Although his strong opinions and his earnest desire to maintain what he believes to be the right side of every great controversy have naturally brought him into frequent antagonism with the representatives of many an important case, I do not know of any public man who has made fewer enemies or who is more generally spoken of with respect and admiration. A man must have very high conceit indeed of his own knowledge and his own judgment who does not feel that he has a great deal to learn from conversation with a master of so many subjects. Yet Bryce never oppresses a listener, as some intellectual leaders are apt to do, with a sense of the listener's inferiority, and the least gifted among us is encouraged to express himself with frankness and freedom while discoursing with Bryce on any question which happens to come up. I think that among his many remarkable qualities is that sincere belief which was characteristic of Mr. Gladstone, and for which Gladstone did not always get due credit—the belief that every man, however moderate his intellectual qualifications, has something to tell which the wisest would be the better for knowing. We must all of us have met scholars and thinkers and political leaders whose inborn sense of their own capacity had an overbearing and even oppressive effect on the ordinary mortal, and made him shy of expressing himself fully lest he should only be displaying his ineptitude or his ignorance in such a presence. But there is nothing of this to be observed in the genial ways of James Bryce, and the listener finds himself unconsciously brought for the time to the level of the master and emboldened to give free utterance to his own ideas and opinions.

Bryce has been made a member of most of the great intellectual and educational institutions of the world, has held degrees and honors of various kinds from the universities of Europe and the United States, and could hardly travel anywhere abroad or at home without finding himself in recognized association with some school of learning in every place where he makes a stay. The freemasonry of intellect and education all over the world gives him rank among its members, and receives him with a welcome recognition wherever he goes. I presume that in the political sphere of action he is henceforward likely to find his congenial career, but he must always have the knowledge that, if for any reason he should give up his political occupation, he can at any moment return to some pursuit in which he has already won an established fame. There are not many political leaders of our time about whom the same could fairly be said. For myself I may frankly say that I hope James Bryce will henceforward devote himself especially to that political career in which he has accomplished such great things. English public life cannot well afford to lose his services just now or for some time to come. A man who can bring to political work such resources of thought and of experience, who can look beneath the surface and above the mere phrases and catchwords of political parties, who can see that Liberalism in its true sense must mean progress, and who can at the same time see clearly for himself what progress really means, and in what direction and by what methods it is to be made—such a man could ill be spared by the Liberalism of our generation. The historical work he has already done is, in its way, complete and imperishable. But the Liberal party has yet to recover its place and to regain the leadership of England's political life. Every effort the Conservatives in office have lately been making to hold their full mastery over the country has shown more and more clearly that they have not kept up with the movements of thought and are not able to understand the true requirements of the time. On the other hand, the limp and shattered condition of the existing Liberal party only shows the absolute necessity for the recognized leadership of men who understand the difference between the work of guiding the country and the ignoble function of competing for power by imitation and by compromise. In the new effort now so sorely needed to create once more a true Liberal party, the country requires, above all things else, the constant service of such men as James Bryce.

*Photograph copyright by London Stereoscopic Co.*
**SIR HENRY CAMPBELL-BANNERMAN**

# SIR HENRY CAMPBELL-BANNERMAN

Sir Henry Campbell-Bannerman has but lately come to hold that position in the House of Commons and in the political world which those who knew him well always believed him destined to attain. He is now not merely the nominal leader of the Liberal Opposition in the House of Commons, but he is universally regarded as one of the very small number of men who could possibly be chosen for the place. Sir William Harcourt and Mr. John Morley are the only Liberal members of the House who could compare with Sir Henry Campbell-Bannerman for influence with the Liberal party, the House of Commons, and the general public. Yet the time is not far distant when he was commonly regarded in the House as a somewhat heavy, not to say stolid, man, one of whom nothing better could be said than that he would probably be capable of quiet, steady work in some subordinate department. I remember well that when Campbell-Bannerman was appointed Chief Secretary to the Lord-Lieutenant of Ireland in 1884, a witty Irish member explained the appointment by the suggestion that Gladstone had made use of Campbell-Bannerman on the principle illustrated by the employment of a sand-bag as part of the defenses of a military fort. Campbell-Bannerman has, in fact, none of the temperament which makes a man anxious to display himself in debate, and whenever, during his earlier years of Parliamentary life, he delivered a speech in the House of Commons, his desire seemed to be to get through the task as quickly as possible and be done with it. He appears to be a man of a naturally reserved habit, with indeed something of shyness about him, and a decided capacity for silence wherever there is no pressing occasion for speech, whether in public or in private.

Many whom I knew were at one time inclined to regard Campbell-Bannerman as a typical specimen of his Scottish compatriots, who are facetiously said to joke with difficulty. As a matter of fact, Campbell-Bannerman has a keen and delightful sense of humor, and can illustrate the weakness of an opponent's case, better than some recognized wits could do, by a few happy touches of sarcasm. He is in every sense of the word a strong man, and, like some other strong men, only seems to know his own strength and to be capable of putting it into action when hard fortune has brought him into political difficulties through which it appears well-nigh impossible that he can make his way. Schiller's hero declares that it must be night before his star can shine, and although Campbell-Bannerman is not quite so poetic and picturesque a figure as Wallenstein, yet I think he might fairly comfort himself by some such encouraging reflection. He had gone through a long and hard-working career in the House of Commons before the world came to know anything of his strength, his judgment, and his courage. He got his education at the University of Glasgow and afterwards at Trinity College, Cambridge, and he obtained a seat in the House of Commons for a Scottish constituency as a Liberal when he was still but a young man. He has held various offices in Liberal administrations. He was Secretary to the Admiralty in 1882, and was Chief Secretary to the Lord-Lieutenant of Ireland for a short time a little later. There is not much to be said about his Irish administration. He governed the country about as well as any English Minister could have done under such conditions, for this was before Gladstone and the Liberal party had been converted to the principle of Home Rule for Ireland; and, at all events, he made himself agreeable to those Irishmen with whom he came into contact by his unaffected manners and his quiet good humor. When Gladstone took office in 1886, Campbell-Bannerman became Secretary for War, and he held the same important position in Gladstone's Ministry of 1892.

The story of that administration tells of a most important epoch in the career of Gladstone and the fortunes of the Liberal party. In 1893 Gladstone brought in his second Home Rule measure for Ireland. His first measure of Home Rule was introduced in 1886, and was defeated in the House of Commons by means of a coalition between the Liberal secessionists and the Conservative Opposition. The Liberal secessionists in the House of Commons, as most of my readers will remember, were led by Joseph Chamberlain. Then there came an interval of Conservative government, and when Gladstone returned to power in 1892 he introduced before long his second measure of Home Rule. The second measure was in many ways a distinct improvement on the first, and in the meantime some of the Liberal secessionists, including Sir George Trevelyan, whose opposition was directed only against certain parts of the first measure, had returned to their allegiance and were ready to give Gladstone all the support in their power for his second attempt. The Home Rule measure was carried through the House of Commons by what we call a substantial although not a great majority, and then it had to go to the House of Lords. Everybody knew in advance what its fate must be in the hereditary chamber. Every great measure of genuine political reform is certain to be rejected in the first instance by the House of Lords. This is the old story, and is repeated again and again with monotonous iteration. The House of Lords always gives way in the end, when the pressure of public opinion from without makes it perilous for the hereditary legislators to maintain their opposition. Therefore the Liberals in general were not much disconcerted by the defeat of the Home Rule measure in the House of Lords. Home Rule for Ireland had been sanctioned by the decisive vote of the House of Commons, and the general impression was that it would only have to be brought in again and perhaps again, according to the usual process with all reform measures, until the opposition of the Lords had been completely borne down. But before the introduction of the second Home Rule measure, some events had taken place which made a great change in the condition of Irish political affairs and put fresh difficulties in the way of Gladstone's new administration.

The Parnell divorce case came on, and led to a serious division in the ranks of the Irish National party and in Irish public opinion. The great majority of Parnell's followers refused to regard him as their leader any longer, and those who determined to support him and to follow him through thick and thin were but a very small minority. Gladstone was firmly convinced, as were the majority of the Irish Nationalist members, that Parnell ought to retire, for a time at least, from the leadership of his party, if not indeed from public life, and keep aloof from active politics until the scandal of the divorce court should have been atoned for by him and should have passed to some extent from public memory. Gladstone was convinced that if Parnell remained the leader of the Irish party it would be almost impossible to arouse in the British constituencies any enthusiasm in the cause of Home Rule strong enough to bring back the Liberals to power and to carry a Home Rule measure. This was a reasonable and practical view of the question, but Parnell and his followers resented it as a positive insult, and Parnell issued a manifesto denouncing Gladstone, the immediate result of which was that break-up of the Home Rule party I have already mentioned. Not very long after came Parnell's early death. It may well be supposed that such events as these must have made a deep and discouraging impression on Gladstone's hopes for the success of the second Home Rule measure. The Irish National party had been broken up for the time, and some even of Gladstone's colleagues in office had allowed themselves to be mastered by the old familiar idea that as Irishmen could not be brought to agree for long on any plan of action, it was futile for English Liberals to put themselves to any inconvenience for the sake of an Irish National cause. Such men might have found it difficult to point out any great measure of political reform in England concerning which the English people had always been in absolute agreement and about which there was no conflict of angry emotion in any section of English representatives. But the fact remained all the same that the dispute in the Irish party had brought a chill to the zeal of many influential English Liberals for the Home Rule cause, and we have had in much more recent days abundant evidence that the chilling influence is with them still.

Among Gladstone's official colleagues there were some who held that the time had come when an appeal ought to be made to the country by means of a dissolution and a general election against the domination of the House of Lords. This appears to have been the opinion of Gladstone himself. Others of his colleagues, however, held back from such an issue, and contended that the moment did not seem favorable for an appeal to the country on the distinct question of Irish Home Rule. The general impression on the public mind was that the decision of the Cabinet was certain to be in favor of an appeal to the country on the one issue or the other, and much surprise was felt when it began to be more and more evident that the Government intended to go on with the ordinary business of the State, as if nothing had happened. The outer world has as yet had no means of knowing what the reasons or the influences were which induced Gladstone and his colleagues to come to this determination. The whole truth will probably never be known until John Morley's "Life of Gladstone" shall make its appearance. We may safely assume in the meantime that Gladstone had the best of reasons for taking the course which he adopted, and that he would have made an appeal to the country against the decision of the House of Lords if he had believed the conditions were favorable for such a challenge just then. Probably Gladstone knew only too well that even among his own colleagues there were some who were turning cold upon the question of Home Rule, who had never accepted his views on that subject with whole-hearted willingness, and could not have been relied upon as steadfast adherents in the struggle. I think I shall be fully justified by any revelations which history or biography has yet to make, when I say that Campbell-Bannerman was among those who would have faithfully followed the great leader to the very last in whatever struggle he had made up his mind to engage. There were, of course, many others of Gladstone's colleagues—men like Sir William Harcourt and John Morley and James Bryce—on whom their leader could have safely reckoned for the same unswerving fidelity and courage. But, whatever were the reasons, there was no appeal made to the country, and the administration went on with its ordinary work in a dull, mechanical fashion. The effect upon the Liberal party was most depressing. Men could not understand why nothing decisive had been done, and at the same time were haunted by a foreboding that some great change was impending over the Liberal party.

The foreboding soon came to be justified. On the 1st of March, 1894, Gladstone delivered his last speech in the House of Commons. The speech dealt with the action of the House of Lords on a subject of comparatively slight importance. The Lords had rejected a measure dealing with the constitution of parish councils, which had been passed by the House of Commons. Gladstone spoke with severity in condemnation of the course taken by the House of Lords. Towards the close of his speech he said: "My duty terminates with calling the attention of this House to a fact which it is really impossible to set aside, that we are considering a part—an essential and inseparable part—of a question enormously large, a question which has become profoundly a truth, a question that will demand a settlement, and must at an early date receive that settlement, from the highest authority." No one who was present in the House when this declaration was made is ever likely to lose the memory of the scene, although not all or even most of those then present quite realized the full significance of Gladstone's words. There were many in the House who did not at once understand that in the words I have quoted the greatest Parliamentary leader of modern times was speaking his farewell to public life. I remember well that a few moments after Gladstone had finished his speech I met John Morley in one of the lobbies, and I asked him if this was really to be taken as the close of Gladstone's career, and he told me, with as much composure as he could command, that in that speech we had heard the last of Gladstone's Parliamentary utterances. That was indeed a memorable day in the history of England, and a day at least equally memorable in the history of Ireland.

I have had to dwell for a while on these historical facts, facts of course known already to all my readers, as a prelude to the most important passages in the Parliamentary career of Campbell-Bannerman. When Gladstone resigned office and withdrew from public life, the question of reconstituting the Liberal administration had to be taken into account. There could be no doubt whatever that the Liberal administration had been much weakened and even discredited by the manner in which it had put up with the domineering action of the House of Lords. The effect on public opinion was all the greater and the more disheartening because it was generally understood that the absence of any such action must have been due to the fact that some of Gladstone's leading colleagues were not prepared to sustain him in the policy he was anxious to carry out. There was therefore a state of something like apathy in the minds of advanced Radicals with regard to any arrangements which seemed likely to be made for the reconstruction of the Ministry. The new administration was formed under the leadership of Lord Rosebery, as Prime Minister, in the House of Lords, and that of Sir William Harcourt, as Chancellor of the Exchequer, in the House of Commons. There can be little doubt that the composition of the new Ministry was regarded as unsatisfactory by the more advanced Liberals in and outside Parliament. The Liberal party is never of late years quite content with an administration which has its Prime Minister in the House of Lords. The real work must always be done in the House of Commons, and it is obviously most inconvenient that the leader of the Government should be one whose position will not allow him to have a seat in the representative chamber. The condition of things is something like that of an army whose Commander-in-Chief can never make his appearance in the encampment or take part in any of the great battles. Even at that time Lord Rosebery, although a most brilliant debater and a capable administrator, was beginning to be regarded as one whose Liberalism was somewhat losing color and whose whole heart was by no means in the advanced policy of Gladstone. There was nothing better to be done, however, at the time than to make the most of the altered conditions, and the new Ministry went to work as well as it could. Campbell-Bannerman, as Secretary for War, had an opportunity of proving his genuine capacity for the duties of his important office. He introduced a new and complete scheme of army reform, which, among other and even more important changes, proposed to bring about the retirement of the Duke of Cambridge from the post of Commander-in-Chief. The Duke of Cambridge was even then a man far advanced in years, who had never in his life shown any real capacity for the work of commanding an army, and whose chief recommendation for so great a position must have been found in the fact that he was a member of the royal family. The new measure was making its way steadily enough through the House of Commons, and every one was beginning to see that in Campbell-Bannerman the country had found an administrator of a very high order. Suddenly, however, the progress of the measure was interrupted by what seemed to be at first only a trivial accident, of which the public in general were inclined to take but little account. The army reform scheme had arrived at what is known as the committee stage of its progress.

I do not desire to occupy the attention of my readers more than is actually necessary with the mere technical details of Parliamentary procedure, and I shall only explain that when a Bill reaches the committee stage its general principle must have been already accepted by the majority in the House, and the House then forms itself into Committee for the purpose of discussing the mere details of the proposed arrangements. During one of the sittings a Conservative member proposed a motion declaring that the Government, or at least the War Office, had not made proper provision for the supply of the material of cordite to the army. This was so purely a technical question, concerning which only soldiers and scientific men could be supposed to have had any means of forming an opinion, that the House troubled itself very little about the whole discussion. But when the House came to take a division on the proposal, the Government was defeated by a majority of seven. This defeat produced at first only a very slight effect on the House in general. During the committee stage of a measure it is quite a matter of ordinary occurrence that a Ministry should be defeated on some question of mere arrangement and detail, and very few in the House of Commons suspected on that occasion that such a vote was likely to bring with it an important Parliamentary crisis. Campbell-Bannerman, however, took a very different view of the event. He appears to have made up his mind that the decision of the House was a distinct vote of censure on his administration, and that he could not continue to hold office after so marked a declaration of disapproval. Now, it may be taken for granted that Campbell-Bannerman was not merely actuated by any personal feeling, by any sense of mere grievance to himself, when he made up his mind to this resolve. He saw clearly that the Government had lost the confidence and the support of the country, and that the sooner the whole futile attempt at administration under such conditions came to an end the better it would be for the business of the State. He knew perfectly well that the Liberal administration was falling to pieces, that its leading members were no longer inspired alike by one great policy, that some of its leaders had ceased to be Liberals in the traditional meaning of the word, and that sooner or later the catastrophe must come. Those of Campbell-Bannerman's colleagues who were as genuine and stanch Liberals as he soon came into agreement with him as to the course that ought to be pursued, and it was known before long in the House of Commons that the Liberal Ministers had resigned their offices and that the long-postponed appeal to the country was to be made at last. Thus for the first time it became known to the public that Campbell-Bannerman was already a power in political life.

Parliament was dissolved and the appeal to the country was made at the general election which necessarily followed. Few Liberals had the slightest doubt as to the result of the appeal. Some of the very measures introduced by the fallen Government which had the strong approval of many advanced Liberals had put certain powerful interests and classes against those who represented this policy. Sir William Harcourt's "death duties" had aroused the indignation of rich men here, there, and everywhere. The measures which the same statesman had endeavored to carry for putting the liquor trade under the control of "local option" had turned the publicans into an organized opposition against Liberal administrators. The result of the general election was the defeat of the Liberal party, and the formation of a Conservative Government with Lord Salisbury at its head holding office as Prime Minister and Foreign Secretary at once, and with Arthur Balfour as First Lord of the Treasury and leader of the House of Commons. The Liberals were weakened in every sense, not merely by the fact that they had come back to Parliament no longer as a Government but only as an Opposition. They were rendered by their internal divisions too weak for effective work as an Opposition. Lord Rosebery continued for the time to act as leader of the Liberal party, while Sir William Harcourt of course became leader of the Opposition in the House of Commons. It soon was quite clear that the Liberal party could not work together so far as its leaders were concerned. It was evident that men like Harcourt and John Morley and Campbell-Bannerman could not act in any cordial union with Lord Rosebery and those Liberals who accepted Lord Rosebery's policy. The result of all this was that Lord Rosebery resigned the leadership of the party and has ever since seemed inclined to start a Liberal party of his own, and that Sir William Harcourt did not believe he was likely to receive such a united support in the House of Commons as would enable him to maintain the leadership of the party with any satisfaction to himself or the country. Harcourt therefore ceased to hold that position; and now came for the first time the opportunity for Campbell-Bannerman. He was chosen leader of the Liberal party in the House of Commons, and he had before him, under all the conditions, a task which might well have seemed hopeless. Lord Rosebery has, from that time to this, delivered speeches all over the country which could only be interpreted as the expression of his desire to call into being a new Liberal party professing a political creed differing in its main characteristics from that which had been proclaimed and carried on by Gladstone. Rosebery renounced Home Rule for Ireland, and refused to act on Gladstone's principles with regard to the protection of Christians in the East against the alternating tyranny and neglect of the Ottoman Government.

Never within my recollection had any leader of a Liberal party in the House of Commons come into a position of such difficulty and disheartenment as that which Campbell-Bannerman had now to maintain. It has often been the lot of the Liberal party to come into the House of Commons with diminished numbers, and have to carry on as best it could be done the battle against a Conservative Government of overwhelming numerical strength. But the peculiar trouble which beset Campbell-Bannerman was that he could not count upon the allegiance of all his nominal followers. He knew that so long as he showed himself determined to maintain the policy of Gladstone he could reckon without fear on the support of such men as Harcourt and John Morley and Bryce. But there were able men among those who occupied the front bench of Opposition on whom he could not always count, men who were publicly displaying themselves as the political associates or followers of Lord Rosebery. Campbell-Bannerman went boldly and steadfastly on, never faltering in the least. He upheld the time-honored creed of genuine Liberalism, "never doubted clouds would break," and by his words and his bearing inspired with fresh courage many a true Liberal whose faith was not faltering, but whose hopes were sinking low. He proved himself quite equal to the incessant work put upon him by his new position as leader of the Liberal party in the House of Commons. He developed a capacity for debate which only those who knew him well had ever before believed him to possess. During all the wild excitement of Jingoism which followed the movements of the war against the two South African Republics, he never yielded to the temptation which overcame so many other Liberals, the temptation to evade a passing unpopularity by suppressing for the time his opinions on the policy of the war. He must have been sorely tried again and again by the sayings and doings of some who still professed to be members of the Liberal party in Parliament. A new Liberal League was actually formed under the inspiration of Lord Rosebery, and its object apparently was to create a new school of Liberalism which should have nothing to do with the traditions of the party and with the doctrines of men like Gladstone.

Now, if all this had been done in open and avowed antagonism to the existing

Liberal party, Campbell-Bannerman might have had a comparatively easy task to undertake. He could have braced himself to do sturdy battle against the promoters of internal disunion; could have set the whole question plainly and squarely before the Liberal public opinion of the country, and demanded a decisive judgment. But the promoters of the new Liberal League did nothing of the kind. They disclaimed any intention to create disunion in the party. They declared that they were the very best of Liberals, and that nothing could exceed their loyalty to the elected leaders of the Liberal party, and protested that in whatever they did they were only trying to help and not to hinder the work of these leaders. When one of the seceders, or supposed seceders, delivered a speech at some public meeting in which he appeared to repudiate the main principles of the Liberal creed, and an open split in the party seemed to be imminent, some other member of the Liberal League hastened to explain that the meaning of his noble friend or his right honorable colleague had been totally misunderstood. He insisted that the only motive of the previous orator was to promote the cordial union of the Liberal party, and, to paraphrase the words of the medical student in "Pickwick" after his quarrel with a fellow-student, that he rather preferred Campbell-Bannerman to his own brother.

Campbell-Bannerman took all these performances with serene good humor. As I have already said, those who know him are well aware that he has a keen, quiet sense of humor, and I feel sure that he must often have been much amused by the odd vagaries of those who would neither fall into the ranks nor admit that they wanted to keep out of the ranks. He has gone steadily on as he began since it became his duty to lead the Liberal Opposition in the House of Commons. He has done the work of leader honorably, patiently, consistently, and fearlessly, and he is recognized as leader by all true Liberals, English, Scotch, and Welsh. He has never fallen away in the slightest degree from the principles of Gladstone where Home Rule and the other just claims of the Irish people are concerned. He has kept the Liberal flag flying, and the whole Liberalism of the country is already beginning to rally round him and to recognize his leadership. Increasing responsibility has only developed in him new capacity to maintain the responsible place. We may well believe that he is destined to do great service yet to the Liberal cause, and to win an honorable place in British history. When he first became leader of the Liberal party in the House of Commons, he might almost have seemed to be the leader of a lost cause, but he has fought the fight bravely and will see the victory before long.

Lector House believes that a society develops through a two-fold approach of continuous learning and adaptation, which is derived from the study of classic literary works spread across the historic timeline of literature records. Therefore, we aim at reviving, repairing and redeveloping all those inaccessible or damaged but historically as well as culturally important literature across subjects so that the future generations may have an opportunity to study and learn from past works to embark upon a journey of creating a better future.

This book is a result of an effort made by Lector House towards making a contribution to the preservation and repair of original ancient works which might hold historical significance to the approach of continuous learning across subjects.

**HAPPY READING & LEARNING!**

LECTOR HOUSE LLP
E-MAIL: lectorpublishing@gmail.com

CPSIA information can be obtained
at www.ICGtesting.com
Printed in the USA
BVHW041342250722
642940BV00003B/227

9 789356 140486